THE FRUIT OF UNFORGIVENESS

SECTION ONE: THE CASE STUDIES

SECTION TWO: THE CURE

THE FRUIT OF UNFORGIVENESS

Copyright © 2017 by Dr Chibueze Ukaegbu.

DEDICATION

This Book is dedicated to our **Lord Jesus Christ**
Who taught us by His Examples the
Beauty of forgiveness.

My prayer is that **The Holy Spirit** will find this Book
as a good building material fit for use
in the building of God's House,
Even The Church.

PREFACE

Many people today are carrying heavy loads in their hearts, loads of hatred, bitterness and the spirit of unforgiveness. They are so overwhelmed by these loads so much so that they become consumed by the desire to exact some form of revenge and vengeance on those they perceive have wronged them.

Dr Chibueze Ukaegbu, in this Book, has sounded a timely alarm, warning us that the spirit of unforgiveness is nothing but destruction to those that harbour it. Starting from the life of Cain, the son of Adam, to Prophet Jonah, he shows that, no matter the source of and the reason for your bitterness (as he enunciates from the different causes of offense in the ten characters he laid bare in the book), the end result, if not properly taken care of as a Child of God, will be destruction.

He did not only bring out the destruction of ten men that allowed the spirit of unforgiveness to rule their lives, but also delves into how we can be delivered from this dangerous spirit. His classical treatment of how the Lord Jesus fulfilled the roles of the two goats in The Day Of Atonement rituals, having suffered greatly to earn us forgiveness with the Father and also granted us the enablement to be able to forgive others, is a must read for everyone.

He beckons on us to take a cue from Joseph, the son of Jacob, as an example of how possible it is for us to forgive those that offended us.

One of our greatest lessons from this book, is the fact that we will be doing ourselves untold great favour by forgiving whatsoever wrong done to us. If not, we will be heading for self-generated destruction.

I recommend this book as a must read for every Christian that wants to live and follow in the Footsteps of Our Master and Saviour Jesus Christ, who in Luke 23 verse 34, showed us the way to live a life of forgiveness, by His First Word on the Cross "Father forgive them for they do not know what they do".

God bless you as you read this book.

Most Rev. Dr. Ignatius C.O. Kattey
Dean Emeritus, Church of Nigeria (Anglican Communion)
Archbishop, Province of Niger Delta
Bishop, Diocese of Niger Delta North
Grand Patron, Scripture Union (Nigeria).

FORWARD

This book exposes the hidden canker of anger, hatred, envy and unforgiveness in human nature and its devastating consequence on an individual. What is considered as causal envy or unforgiveness when harboured and nurtured over a long period of time tends to breed bitterness, eventually wrecking havoc and affecting the individual and others in undesirable ways.

It is a divine principle taught by our Lord Jesus himself that we are forgiven our trespasses only on condition that we forgive others their offenses against us.

The Lord considers this principle important enough to include it in 'The Lord's Prayer' (Matt 6:12-15).

The writer, in each chapter unfolds a wide variety of cases in the Holy Bible involving anger, envy, bitterness, evil plots etc. and its consequences. As one would see in this book, a seemingly casual envy or rivalry if not checked from the beginning blinds the perpetuator's perspective and objective sense. This usually driven by fury may lead to a dire consequence of murder in the extreme. It is therefore not surprising to read from the Gospel our Lord Jesus' word describing anger as murderous. Anyone engaging in such acts would be in danger of hell fire and judgment (Matt 5:21-22).

All who desire to live godly lives and be well pleasing to the Lord will find this book priceless. A rare opportunity of reading with classic examples from the Holy Scriptures condensed together in a single exposition on the effects of anger and bitterness for our learning.

The rich analysis of the cases and the wealth of information revealed in this book may serve as a mirror in which one may find traits of one's inward vulnerabilities; to the hungry soul this is grace and also the goodness of the Lord. You cannot help but be led to repentance after reading this book.

The book deals with applications in our Christian journey, in the home and our daily walk with God.

I am confident that, in reading this book, you would be left with a deep impression of the liberties that can be experienced in living an 'anger-free' and forgiving life; leaving you free to serve the Lord and walk well-pleasing of the Lord.

May the Lord grant you open hearts and minds and may He Himself navigate you in the reading of each section this book, and grant you necessary light for your walk with Him in full obedience to His word.

Brother Daniel Nunoo
Former Chairman/Managing Director, Shell Petroleum, Accra.
GHANA.

COMMENTS

Unforgiveness: This is the bane, behind our unsuccessful Christian living today. This book is timely. It is good for every Christian. Both young and old. We must forgive, so that we will also enjoy forgiveness, from our Father in Heaven.

AUSTIN OKOSUN, Benin City, Nigeria

I found this a commendable piece of work which confirms that the Lord has yet more light and truth to break forth from His word. And as such, we should not limit the truth of God to our poor reach of mind. Therefore, whatever is written is for our admonition that we may learn from the errors of those who have gone before us.

The sin of unforgiveness, how grievous! We don't seem to consider its weight a bit. Here, we are helped to see the repercussions of being vindictive and not letting go offenses. It is quite instructive that going through history not one of those who trod this dangerous path of unforgiving spirit survived it. All without exception paid dearly with their lives. What a tragedy!

We all need to learn that at the close of each day, all our accounts with God and with one another will be settled. Then we can sleep in the joyful awareness that there is not a cloud between us and God. No bank ever closes its business day until its balance sheet is absolutely correct. So no true child of God should close a single day until his accounts with God and man have been thoroughly reconciled.

Praise the Lord for the divine provision given to us through His redemptive work!

RAYMOND AYEDUN, Benin City, Nigeria

I will be honest with you; the Introduction of this book alone raised my interest. It attracts me when a writing is based purely on the Holy Scriptures and not merely on man's opinion or observation. Beginning from Genesis and traversing the old and new testaments to reveal the way of God in handling or dealing with unforgiveness in the heart of His people is a worthwhile labour.

I believe we need this more than before in the body of Christ as we sense the Lord rounding up this dispensation and also because the topic chosen is a sin harboured most times even by supposedly spiritual men; one of the last infirmity even of noble souls - unforgiveness.

I hope that we can use the contents of this book to guide the saints in our localities.

May the stamp of the Holy Spirit, without which any labour is in vain, be upon this book and may the people of God be edified. Amen

COMMENTS

CLEMENT SIYANBOLA, Lagos, Nigeria.

I have read the book and I must say that it really touched the heart of the topic.

First, through all the examples in the Bible about unforgiveness, we can only conclude with the saying in Galatians which says "Do not be deceived, God is not mocked; for whatever a man sows, that he will also reap" - Gal. 6:7. Over and over again, the spirit of unforgiveness has swallowed up all men and women, regardless of their age, race, and spiritual maturity. May the Lord deliver us from this evil spirit and give us a heart like His.

The second point is that to forgive is really a matter of choice as shown in this book. Joseph is a very good example. Even though he was wronged by his brothers, he still forgave them and that gave him victory to become the highest person in Egypt next to Pharaoh. If Joseph had not forgiven his brothers, he would not have reigned. Joseph could have chosen to nurture hatred and unforgiveness but he didn't.

The third point is that God is the God of Forgiveness. The Psalmist said "If You, Lord, should mark iniquities, O Lord, who could stand? But there is forgiveness with You, That You may be feared." Psalm 130:3-4. Just imagine the debt of the whole world, how great a sin mankind had committed over the ages but God still forgave us all our sins by giving up His only begotten son to die for our sake. Hallelujah! God forgave all our sins! 1 Tim. 1:15 say "Here is a trustworthy saying that deserves full acceptance: Christ Jesus came into the world to save sinners--of whom I am the worst". Even though I did not deserve to be forgiven, God still forgave me and He forgave you and all that accept and appropriate to themselves the redemptive work of our Lord Jesus Christ. This book highlighted the painful route Lord Jesus went through in order to obtain our forgiveness.

This brings me to the fourth point. The very foundation of our Christian life is based on us being forgiven. No wonder this was found in the Lord's Prayer that He taught his disciples. The Lord's Prayer instructed us in Luke 11:4a "And forgive us our sins, for we also forgive everyone who is indebted to us". You enter the Christian life through forgiveness, you stay in the Christian life through forgiveness and even when you're martyred for the Lord, you end through forgiveness.

I highly recommend this book to every Christian to prayerfully read this book and ask the Lord to fill us all with Himself who is the very forgiveness in us.

ADEWALE OBASEKI, Accra, Ghana.

ACKNOWLEDGEMENT

I want to acknowledge with gratitude and thanks to God who inspired and strengthened me to write this Book.

I want to acknowledge the immense contribution of my wife of nearly 40 years, Victoria and our children, Uzodinma, Kelechi, Tomiwa, Oge, Chibueze Jnr, Osese, Chike, Lanre, Onyi and Chidu for their various contributions and encouragement in putting my ideas to paper. I want to additionally thank Kelechi for suggesting the title of this book, Chike for his contribution in making the Cover Page, Chibueze Jnr and my wife Victoria for reading and correcting the first manuscript.

I want to specially thank Archbishop Ignatius Kattey, the Dean Emeritus of the Anglican Communion, Nigeria, for the amazing roles he played in my Christian life right from our days as students in College of Science and Technology, Port Harcourt, Nigeria, till now. I want to also thank him for finding time in his busy schedule to read the manuscript and write the Preface to this Book.

I want to thank my brother Daniel Nunoo, the retired Chairma/Managing Director of Shell Petroleum, Ghana/Cote D'Ivore for taking time to read the manuscript and pen the Forward to this Book.

My many thanks go to Kevaughn Isaacs, a graphic designer of note, for crafting the final design of the Cover Page.

I will not forget to thank Edirin Edewor whose webinar and subsequent interactions with me paved the way for the publishing of this Book through Amazon.

My thanks also go to Ini Akpan and her company for painstakingly proofreading the entire manuscript, editing and producing the masterpiece that the Book turned out to become.

Please accept my thanks, Rich Stephenson and his dear wife, Rachael, for inviting me over to their home in Coventry, England, and for the opportunity I had in sharing my thoughts about this Book with him and his insightful contributions thereafter.

My immense thanks and gratitude go to Jerry Okine, Austin Okosun, Osita Ogbonnaya, Daniel Oputa, Clement Siyanbola, Raymond Ayedun, Xavier Usen, Dr Austin Akalonu and Adewale Obaseki for their wonderful and thoughtful comments and contributions towards the completion of this Book.

Finally, I want to acknowledge with thanks members of Church in Aba for standing with me in prayers and for their untiring support all through the journey of writing this Book.

ACKNOWLEDGEMENT

MAY THE ALMIGHTY GOD ABUNDANTLY BLESS YOU ALL IN JESUS NAME, AMEN.

TABLE OF CONTENTS

TABLE OF CONTENTS

CHAPTER 1

INTRODUCTION

Romans 12 : 21 (KJV)
²¹ Be not overcome of evil, but overcome evil with good

Hatred, bitterness and an unforgiving spirit are terrible cankerworms that destroy the human system of those who harbour them. Today, many people live lives led by an unforgiving spirit, lives of hatred. They are virtually walking corpses because most of their time and knowledge is devoted towards planning to avenge the evil meted to them or their loved ones.

I share the stories of Bible characters who let an unforgiving spirit eat them up and the awful destruction it brought to them in this book. I analysed each character carefully beginning with Cain, son of Adam. In the following chapters, you will read about ten cases, which I considered in each chapter.

Chapter 2 –
Cain, the son of Adam: Jealous of God's Blessing on Another

Cain was jealous of God's blessing on Abel, his brother. He was resentful because God accepted his brother's sacrifice and not his. Unfortunately, instead of seeking out the way to attract God's blessing, he allowed an unforgiving spirit overwhelm him and he killed the object of God's blessing.

Chapter 3 –
Simeon and Levi, sons of Jacob: Angry over the Ill-treatment of a Loved One

Simeon and Levi were both so angry over the treatment Ahimelech meted to their sister, Diana that they took it upon themselves to revenge the offender and his people without their father's

1

knowledge or permission. As a result, they ended up attracting curses from their father that followed them down to generations unborn. It was terrible.

Chapter 4 –
Korah the Levite: Thought of Himself More Highly Than Others

Korah considered himself to be higher than others whom God placed in positions of authority. He became so angry that he decided to overturn the applecart. Sadly, he ended up being swallowed by the earth together with all whom he drew into his rebellion.

Chapter 5 –
Abimelech, Son of Gideon: Nursed Hurts over Years while Biding Time

Abimelech, the son of Gideon's concubine, harboured hurts over many years. This hurt caused an unforgiving spirit to overwhelm him and lead him to the killing of his father's children. At the end of it all, he was also killed by a woman who crushed his head with a milling stone.

Chapter 6 –
Saul, First King of Israel: Had an Unforgiving Spirit Born of Misplaced Aggression

Saul had misplaced aggression for David, who had played no part whatsoever in the source of his anger and malice. He went after David with intent to kill him because the women had lavished praises on him. He was destroyed in the end – he committed suicide.

Chapter 7 –
Joab, Commander of David's Army: Embittered by His Failures to Do the Right Thing

INTRODUCTION

Joab was embittered by his inability to nip a potential source of danger at the bud and lost his brother as a result. His anger and bitterness intensified at his brother's death. This led him to avenge his brother's death by killing Abner. Although Joab was David's nephew and Solomon's cousin, that did not save him from the fruit of an unforgiving spirit as he was killed by Solomon. Sadly, such a great warrior and a great commander was destroyed because of his actions.

Chapter 8 –
Ahithophel, the Oracle of God: Felt Insulted by the Evil Action of Another

Ahithophel felt insulted by the immoral action of David because it involved his granddaughter. He decided to avenge even after God had forgiven David. And of course, he was suddenly ruined as he committed suicide as a result of his deeds.

Chapter 9 –
Absalom, Son of David: Accumulated Anger and Hatred over Perceived Inaction

Absalom's case was the release of accumulated anger and hatred over his father's inaction over the evil done to his sister. He was full of venom and exerted revenge on the perpetrator of the evil and on his father as well. He rebelled against his father's authority and of course, ended up being slaughtered like a goat.

Chapter 10 –
Haman, the Agagite: Avenged Generational Hatred

Haman was a harbinger of generational hatred and vengeance. His forefathers, the Amalekites hated the Israelites with passion. As an Agagite, he could not forgive what Saul and Prophet Samuel did to his people, especially his forefather, King Agag. All his life, he was planning ways to annihilate the Jews. The traps he set and the gallows he built for his enemies turned out to be his. He was hung on the gallows alongside his fellow conspirators. That was his fruit of not forgiving.

Chapter 11 –
Jonah the Prophet: Angry over God's Goodness to those He Desired Punished

Jonah was angry at God's goodness and readiness to forgive those whom he harboured generational hatred for – the people of Nineveh. Of course, he could not stop God from exercising His grace and mercy towards the people of Nineveh. Jonah sought death as a result and may have lived a life that was completely without peace and joy and full of regrets.

In the ten cases considered in this book, the result was always destruction. It all comes down to the fact that we need to repent from every root of an unforgiving spirit which we may be sheltering. This is very important and necessary if we desire to live a life free of rancour and the dangers of destruction.

Chapter 12 –
An Unforgiving Spirit in the Home Front

The home front wasn't neglected in this book as I brought to a focus how we allow our marriages degenerate due to an unforgiving spirit; how that person whom we called our sweetheart at the beginning morphed into the devil because we refused to let go. The spirit that fails to forgive in marriage and the family has been a great source of great pain to many homes.

Chapter 13 –
Dealing with an Unforgiving Spirit

In the Gospels, Jesus spoke on the issue of forgiveness and the dangers of an unforgiving spirit various times. In this chapter, efforts were made to use scriptural references to bring to light how to deal with an unforgiving spirit.

Chapter 14 –
Our Salvation – A Beautiful Thing: The Cleansing Power of the Blood of our Lord Jesus

This book is emphatic on the need for us to repent and find the cure for the spirit that fails to forgive. This chapter is therefore dedicated to what our Lord Jesus did for us. It chronicles the route our Lord Jesus passed through in order to obtain forgiveness for our sins from the Father and bring us into His kingdom. The essence of this chapter is to remind us that if Christ could do this for us, we have no reason to scorn forgiveness. It also shows that because our Lord Jesus did it, He can empower us to live a life full of forgiveness.

Chapter 15 –
Why We Should Forgive

This chapter explores the life of Joseph, son of Jacob. It brings to light how he forgave his brothers wholeheartedly despite the evil they had perpetrated against him. Also, it reassures us that if he could live a life that is completely free of bitterness, it's possible to forgive and live a free life.

Chapter 16 –
What Should Be our Response to Hurts and Offenses?

Proverbs 14:9 (God's Word Edition) reads, **"There's forgiveness amongst decent people"**. Surely, there's forgiveness amongst decent people. Anyone with a heart devoid of forgiveness spirit carries a darkened heart about and therefore cannot be a decent person. A heart full of bitterness and desire for revenge is an indecent heart that is devoid of Christ and all He stands for. This chapter encourages us to be decent people.

It is my prayer that you take out time and read this book to the end. You will definitely find the book valuable and encouraging, especially in identifying and dealing with any unforgiving spirit. It will also equip you to help someone deal with such a spirit. Enjoy your read and may the Good Lord bless you as you read. Amen.

SECTION ONE –

The Case Studies

CHAPTER 2

CAIN THE SON OF ADAM
Jealous of God's Blessing on Another

Cain was the first born of Adam, a tiller of the ground and a farmer. At that time, all that the Lord asked man to eat were vegetables; animals were not to be consumed as food. It could also be assumed that Abel was also a farmer and a cattle-rearer but his was for definite spiritual purposes. His purpose for rearing cattle was for sacrifices unto the Lord. So I believe that Abel cultivated the land for his feeding and then for God, he reared cattle.

The record of Cain's rejected sacrifice
"And in process of time it came to pass, that Cain brought of the fruit of the ground an offering unto Jehovah. And Abel, he also brought of the firstlings of his flock and of the fat thereof. And Jehovah had respect unto Abel and to his offering: but unto Cain and to his offering he had not respect. And Cain was very wroth, and his countenance fell." (Gen. 4:3-5)

The facts as recorded by Moses in the book of Genesis are very plain. Both Cain and Abel came to worship before the Lord and both brought a sacrifice. However, there was a difference in what they brought before the Lord. Cain brought a sacrifice of the fruit of the ground. His offering was a bloodless sacrifice. While Abel brought forth a bloody sacrifice and the fat thereof.

CAIN THE SON OF ADAM

The outcome of their offerings before the Lord was that Jehovah respected Abel **and** his offering, but he did not acknowledge Cain **nor** his offering.

Why Was Cain's Sacrifice Rejected?

The Bible is very specific about what they offered:
One offered the produce of the ground and the other offered a bloody sacrifice.

The Book of Hebrews puts it more succinctly:

> "By faith, Abel offered unto God a more excellent sacrifice than Cain, through which he had witness borne to him that he was righteous, God bearing witness in respect of his gifts: and through it he being dead yet speaketh" (Hebrews 11:4).

Abel presented his sacrifice unto the Lord **by faith**. Neither Moses nor the New Testament writers ever mentioned that Cain brought his sacrifice by faith.

Cain's worship was human-driven, what he thought was acceptable and according to what he believed was right. It was his senses and wisdom which dictated to him what God should be pleased to accept as a sacrifice.

There is no doubt that he gave his best; his produce must have been a pleasant sight to behold. He must have worked and laboured over those crops until the harvest. He must have believed that with the effort, time and nourishing he gave his crops, the Lord would surely accept them as a sacrifice.

His rejection elicited a terrible reaction from him because he never expected that all his labour would come to naught.

It is however important to note that Cain's sacrifice was rejected not because he offered terrible products of the ground, nor because he offered them to despise God. Rather, his offering was rejected because he offered according to what he expected God to accept, not according to what God wanted; not by faith.

Faith in this respect, is the result of hearing God's word, submitting the whole being to its dictate and acting in accordance to what the Lord has instructed and wanted.

The Sacrifices of Cain and Abel

During the time of sacrifice, Abel offered a sacrifice of cattle and the blood of sheep unto the Lord while Cain offered fruits of the land. The fruit of the land was unacceptable to God as there must be shedding of blood whenever we come before God to atone for our sins. *Without the shedding of blood there is no forgiveness of sins* (Hebrews 9:24).

Abel offered what was acceptable before God and what God desired. But Cain offered what was right in his own eyes, the fruit of his hands and the fruit of his labour.

When we are dealing with God, what we think is

irrelevant. What is important is what is God saying. What is the thought of God on this issue? That should take pre-eminence over whatsoever we think. Even what we think that God is thinking, which is neither here nor there, is also unacceptable to God. What is acceptable is what is God saying concerning this issue. As far as the issue of coming to Him was concerned, God showed an example by being the first to sacrifice on behalf of man, when he killed an animal and used the skin for a covering for Adam and Eve after they sinned against Him.

This is very well expressed in Hebrews 11 verse 4:

> "By faith Abel offered to God a more excellent sacrifice than Cain, through which he obtained witness that he was righteous, God testifying of his gifts; and through it he being dead still speaks."

They used leaves- the fruit of the land- to cover themselves and God showed by His action that using leaves, a fruit of the ground, was unacceptable to Him. God showed them that there must be shedding of blood for every sin that is committed.

Yet, Cain went ahead to offer the fruit of the ground unlike Abel his brother who took from his cattle, shed blood and offered an acceptable sacrifice unto the Lord. Now this was the case with their sacrifices, one sacrificed to God, not to man.

Abel, we should take note, did not advice Cain on what to use for his sacrifice. No, Abel did not. One will therefore,

11

not say that Abel wronged Cain by deceiving him into giving the wrong sacrifice while he, Abel, used what was acceptable before God for his sacrifice. Each of them did theirs according to their own understanding, perception and decision. It was a personal decision to either follow God or follow man.

Instead of Cain to sit back and think, "Why was my sacrifice rejected? Is there anything that I can do to ameliorate the situation? Can I turn the clock back? Can I cause God to accept my sacrifice? What can I do for God to accept my sacrifice?" He did not do that. He did not think in that direction rather, he became jealous of Abel whose sacrifice was accepted.

That jealously turned to bitterness and the bitterness grew into resentment. He then hatched a plan to avenge his brother for offering an acceptable sacrifice. This is unbelievable. Abel did not wrong him. This is a terrible dimension, an unthinkable dimension of bitterness. Abel did not wrong Cain in any way, he did not. There was no reason for Cain to be angry with Abel. Abel did not tell God not to accept Cain's sacrifice. The sacrifice was not to Abel, so Cain had no reason to be angry with Abel.

The sacrifice was to God; both of them in their own way, sacrificed to God. So if there was anybody Cain should have been angry with, it should have been with God and definitely not with Abel.

Cain should have asked God, "Why did you reject my

sacrifice?" and listened to what God would have told him. But no, he chose to be jealous of his brother.

Cain's Crime

Now God spoke to Cain and said, "What is in your heart is deadly, it is not the way to go; if you go on this way, it will lead you to something terrible." He told him, Behold, sin is at your door. It is knocking at your door. Retrace your steps. If you do the right thing, will you not be acceptable? God had to speak with him. God had to caution him and let him know that there was still a second chance for him to do the right thing and offer an acceptable blood-shed sacrifice.

God gave him an option by telling him there was still a second chance; it was still possible for him to redeem the situation by doing the right thing. But, no, he didn't want to do that. He allowed the resentment he harboured against his brother become so deadly that he waylaid and killed his brother.

God's Judgment

After Cain's vexation towards his brother ran its full course, God demanded of his brother from him. His response to God was, "Am I my brother's keeper?" For rejecting God's given opportunity to redeem his failed sacrifice and for allowing the unforgiving spirit that possessed him run its full course leading to the killing of Abel, Cain came under a very harsh judgment from God.

The Curse of Cain:

God's judgment (or the curse of Cain) is found in Genesis Chapter 4 from verses 10 through 14, in which God confronted Cain about the murder of his brother Abel.

> "[11]And now you are cursed from the ground, which has opened its mouth to receive your brother's blood from your hand. [12]When you work the ground, it shall no longer yield to you its strength. You shall be a fugitive and a wanderer on the earth." [13]Cain said to the LORD, "My punishment is greater than I can bear. [14]Behold, you have driven me today away from the ground and from your face, I shall be hidden. I shall be a fugitive and a wanderer on the earth, and whoever finds me will kill me." (ESV)

Cain's punishment was linked to the fruit of his unforgiving attitude. Cain would no longer be able to cultivate the soil (v.[11-12]) because his brother's blood cried out to God from the ground upon which he was slain (v.[10]). Ironically, God chose to deprive Cain of his primary skill, which was to work as a tiller of the ground (Genesis 4:3), the source of his unacceptable sacrifice that became the source of his resentment towards his brother. God also stated that Cain would be a fugitive and a wanderer on the earth.

Cain protested that the judgment was too much for him. He was completely cut off from God, deprived of his primary occupation of tilling the ground and made a vagabond and a fugitive, running from all and sundry.

The Result On His Lineage

All that came through him became infected with the overflow of Cain's judgment. Mathew Henry in his commentary[1] about what proceeded from Cain is very much on point.

He wrote the following about Cain's race:

> "Genesis 4: 19-24~~ One of Cain's wicked race is the first recorded, as having broken the law of marriage. Hitherto, one man had but one wife at a time but Lamech took two. Worldly things, are the only things that carnal, wicked people set their hearts upon, and are most clever and industrious about. So it was with this race of Cain. Here was a father of shepherds, and a father of musicians, but not a father of the faithful. Here is one to teach about brass and iron, but none to teach the good knowledge of the Lord: here are devices how to be rich, and how to be mighty, and how to be merry; but nothing of God, of his fear and service. Present things fill the heads of most. Lamech had enemies, whom he had provoked. He draws a comparison betwixt himself and his ancestor Cain; and flatters himself that he is much less criminal. He seems to abuse the patience of God in sparing Cain, into an encouragement to expect that he may sin and go unpunished."

Cain's lineage became a lineage of outcasts and everyone

that came from his loins became an outcast, pursuing the pleasures and desires of the flesh without regard for what the desire of God was.

Exclusion Of Cain And His Descendants From The Genealogy Of Adam

It is instructive to note that after Cain allowed himself to be overwhelmed by his jealousy and bitterness towards his brother; he shot himself and his descendants out of the genealogy of Adam.

In chapter 5 of Genesis, Cain was not mentioned in the genealogy of Adam. Cain was not mentioned because he was completely out of the way and I believe it was also because his linage was badly polluted by the unforgiving spirit that had overwhelmed him.

Genesis Chapter 5: 1 – 8 (KJV)

[1]This is the book of the generations of Adam. In the day that God created man, in the likeness of God made he him; [2]Male and female created he them; and blessed them, and called their name Adam, in the day when they were created. [3]And Adam lived an hundred and thirty years, and begat a son in his own likeness, after his image; and called his name Seth: [4]And the days of Adam after he had begotten Seth were eight hundred years: and he begat sons and daughters: [5]And all the days that Adam lived were nine hundred and thirty years: and he died. [6]And Seth lived an hundred and five years, and begat Enos: [7]And Seth lived after he begat Enos eight hundred and seven years, and begat sons and daughters: [8]And all the days of Seth were nine hundred and twelve years: and he died.

CAIN THE SON OF ADAM

He was completely cut off from everything that was godly. This is a case of bearing the burden of an unforgiving spirit. An unforgiving spirit can ruin a man, his lineage and everything that belongs to him.

The source of his bitterness is very interesting. It is a classic case of misplaced aggression.

Save Yourself From Cain's Judgment

There are many times when we get plagued with Cain's disease. Sometimes, we get afflicted by misplaced aggression. We, out of jealousy, can decide to afflict someone that has done nothing to us. Their crime may be that the Lord has blessed them and because we feel left out, we may design and plan ways and means of afflicting them. We may become overwhelmed by envy which can lead to bitterness that could give birth to vengefulness.

If you are in such a situation now, as you begin to plan and articulate ways and means of harming someone that has done nothing to you, know that God is watching you.

As the Lord spoke to Cain warning him of the danger of the road he was allowing the devil lead him through, pleading with him to retrace his step, in that same way, the Spirit of the Lord is talking to you now. If you are in the shoes of Cain at this moment and out of jealousy have become embittered because of the success of somebody else, the Lord is speaking to you now to retrace your steps. The end thereof, if like Cain you refuse to retrace your steps, is destruction. You will destroy yourself. You will destroy your family. You will destroy your lineage. Retrace your steps and ask for forgiveness and the Lord will restore you to life.

CHAPTER 3

SIMEON AND LEVI, SONS OF JACOB.

Angry over the Ill-treatment of a Loved One

Genesis 33: 16 – 20 (KJV)

[16] *So Esau returned that day on his way unto Seir.* [17] *And Jacob journeyed to Succoth, and built him an house, and made booths for his cattle: therefore the name of the place is called Succoth.* [18] *And Jacob came to Shalem, a city of Shechem, which is in the land of Canaan, when he came from Padanaram; and pitched his tent before the city.* [19] *And he bought a parcel of a field, where he had spread his tent, at the hand of the children of Hamor, Shechem's father, for an hundred pieces of money.* [20] *And he erected there an altar, and called it Elelohe-Israel.*

In Genesis chapter 33 verses 16 through 20, we see that after Jacob's encounter with Esau his brother, on his way back from Laban his mother's brother, he came to Shalem, a city of Shechem. The King of the land was Hamor and the Prince of the land was Shechem.

The Folly Of Shechem The Prince

Genesis 34 (KJV)

[1] *And Dinah the daughter of Leah, which she bare unto Jacob, went out to see the daughters of the land.* [2] *And when Shechem the son of Hamor the Hivite, prince of the country, saw her, he took her, and lay with her, and defiled her.* [3] *And his soul clave unto Dinah the daughter of Jacob, and he loved*

19

the damsel, and spake kindly unto the damsel. ⁴And Shechem spake unto his father Hamor, saying, Get me this damsel to wife. ⁵And Jacob heard that he had defiled Dinah his daughter: now his sons were with his cattle in the field: and Jacob held his peace until they were come. ⁶And Hamor the father of Shechem went out unto Jacob to commune with him. ⁷And the sons of Jacob came out of the field when they heard it: and the men were grieved, and they were very wroth, because he had wrought folly in Israel in lying with Jacob's daughter: which thing ought not to be done. ⁸And Hamor communed with them, saying, The soul of my son Shechem longeth for your daughter: I pray you give her him to wife. ⁹And make ye marriages with us, and give your daughters unto us, and take our daughters unto you. ¹⁰And ye shall dwell with us: and the land shall be before you; dwell and trade ye therein, and get you possessions therein. ¹¹And Shechem said unto her father and unto her brethren, Let me find grace in your eyes, and what ye shall say unto me I will give. ¹²Ask me never so much dowry and gift, and I will give according as ye shall say unto me: but give me the damsel to wife. ¹³And the sons of Jacob answered Shechem and Hamor his father deceitfully, and said, because he had defiled Dinah their sister: ¹⁴And they said unto them, We cannot do this thing, to give our sister to one that is uncircumcised; for that were a reproach unto us: ¹⁵But in this will we consent unto you: If ye will be as we be, that every male of you be circumcised; ¹⁶Then will we give our daughters unto you, and we will take your daughters to us, and we will dwell with you, and we will become one people. ¹⁷But if ye will not hearken unto us, to be circumcised; then will we take our daughter, and we will be gone. ¹⁸And their words pleased Hamor and Shechem Hamor's son. ¹⁹And the young man deferred not to do the thing, because he had delight in Jacob's daughter: and he was more honourable than all the house of his father. ²⁰And Hamor and Shechem his son came unto the gate of their city, and communed with the men of their city, saying, [21] These men are peaceable with us; therefore let them dwell in the land, and trade therein; for the land, behold, it is large enough for them; let us take their daughters to us for wives, and let us give them our daughters. [22] Only herein will the men consent unto us for to dwell with us, to be one people, if every male among us be circumcised, as they are circumcised. [23] Shall not their cattle and their substance and every beast of theirs be ours? only let us consent unto them, and they will dwell with us. [24] And unto Hamor and unto Shechem his son hearkened all that went out of the gate of his city; and every male was circumcised, all that went out of the gate of his city. [25] And it came to pass on the third day, when they were sore, that two of the sons of Jacob, Simeon and Levi, Dinah's brethren, took each man his sword, and came upon the city boldly, and slew all the males. [26] And they slew Hamor and Shechem his son with the edge of the sword, and took Dinah out of Shechem's house, and went out. [27] The sons of Jacob came upon the slain, and spoiled the city, because they had defiled their sister. [28] They took their sheep, and their oxen, and their asses, and that which was in the city, and that which was in the field, [29] And all their wealth, and all their little ones, and their wives took they captive, and spoiled even all that was in the house. [30] And Jacob said to Simeon and Levi, Ye have troubled me to make me to stink among the inhabitants of the land, among the Canaanites and the Perizzites: and I being few in number, they shall gather themselves together against me, and slay me; and I shall be destroyed, I and my house. [31] And they said, Should he deal with our sister as with a harlot?

Shechem the Prince saw Dinah- sister of Levi, Simeon, Reuben and Judah, loved her and unfortunately, defiled her. He was very willing to marry her in a proper way. Therefore, he went with his people to see Jacob and his children for necessary marriage rites. They presented themselves and asked for Dinah's hand in marriage to their prince, Shechem.

Simeon and Levi were incensed that Shechem had defiled their sister. The visit of the prince and his people was an opportunity they looked for. The two brothers planned the revenge for the humiliation of their sister by the Prince. They were so embittered and their hearts filled with thirst for revenge that they planned to get back at the entire community and not Shechem alone. The entire community was to pay for the crime that their prince committed against their sister. What a tragedy!

It is instructive to note here, that Dinah was Jacob's daughter. Apart from Simeon and Levi, she was also the sister of four other sons of Leah, Jacob's wife and half sister to five other sons of Jacob at that time.

The Revenge

Now as they connived, they planned something terrible, very terrible against Shechem and against his entire community. A revenge strategy that would hit at Shechem and his people when they would be too incapacitated to fight back. All these plans were without the approval of their father neither did they take their other brothers into confidence.

No one was privy to the evil they had hatched in avenging the defilement of their sister. They told Shechem, his father, Hamor and all that came with them that Shechem could marry their sister under one condition- that all the men of the community, including the prince and king, would be circumcised since an uncircumcised male cannot marry their sister. Nobody knew what evil these two were planning.

Because Shechem was greatly in love with Dinah, he did not only accept the condition but also persuaded his father to accept it. His father called his people and told them that circumcision for the men was the way to go as this would open doors for them to marry the Hebrew daughters and the Hebrews would also marry their daughters. The king further informed his subjects that Jacob was very rich and intermarriage with them would give them access to Jacob's wealth. This sounded very attractive to the people and the men agreed with the king and his son for the mass circumcision of all the men in the community.

The men circumcised themselves as agreed. On the third day, when the pain of the circumcision was at its peak, Simeon and Levi took their swords, went into the city destroyed and killed off all the men, not Shechem alone, but all the men of the land who at this time were incapacitated by the sore circumcision. They wiped out the men and took their wives, girls and cattle as spoil. The destruction was not only massive, but devastating.

The men of this community were wiped out because of the unforgiving spirit in the hearts of these two brothers.

Jacob became scared, so scared of possible repercussions from the actions of his two sons that he had to leave the land with his entire family and journeyed to Bethel. Bethel was where Jacob had met with God on his way to his uncle, Laban.

The Curse That Followed The Revenge

The two young men in their thinking thought they had done a great job by avenging the disgrace that was meted out to their sister but unfortunately, they had planted a seed that was going to bear terrible fruits for both of them.

This seed of resentment normally bears fruit of self-destruction and what happened to them when Jacob on his dying bed, blessed the children of Israel attests to this fact. When it was the turn of Simeon and Levi to receive their blessings from their father, Jacob remembered this terrible incident. This is how the Amplified Version of the Holy Bible narrates Genesis Chapter 49 verses 5 to 7:

> "[5] Simeon and Levi are brothers [equally headstrong, deceitful, vindictive, and cruel]; their swords are weapons of violence and revenge. [6] O my soul, do not come into their secret council; Let not my glory (honor) be united with their assembly [for I knew nothing of their plot]; because in their anger they killed men [an honored man, Shechem, and the Shechemites], And in their self-will they lamed oxen. [7] Cursed be their anger, for it was fierce; And their wrath, for it was cruel. I will divide and disperse them in Jacob, And [d]scatter them in [the midst of the land of] Israel."

SIMEON AND LEVI, SONS OF JACOB

What a blessing! He would divide them in Jacob and scatter them in Israel! That's the fruits of bitterness. Cursed be their anger for it was fierce and their wrath for it was cruel. That was it. They were scattered. Theirs was just destruction; they destroyed, like their father said, an honourable man- Shechem and for that destruction, they hurt themselves badly.

The Blessings Of Moses And The Curse Unabated

Deuteronomy 33 (KJV)

₁ And this is the blessing, wherewith Moses the man of God blessed the children of Israel before his death. ²And he said, The LORD came from Sinai, and rose up from Seir unto them; he shined forth from mount Paran, and he came with ten thousands of saints: from his right hand went a fiery law for them. ³Yea, he loved the people; all his saints are in thy hand: and they sat down at thy feet; every one shall receive of thy words. ⁴Moses commanded us a law, even the inheritance of the congregation of Jacob. ⁵And he was king in Jeshurun, when the heads of the people and the tribes of Israel were gathered together. ⁶Let Reuben live, and not die; and let not his men be few. ⁷And this is the blessing of Judah: and he said, Hear, LORD, the voice of Judah, and bring him unto his people: let his hands be sufficient for him; and be thou an help to him from his enemies. ⁸And of Levi he said, Let thy Thummim and thy Urim be with thy holy one, whom thou didst prove at Massah, and with whom thou didst strive at the waters of Meribah; ⁹Who said unto his father and to his mother, I have not seen him; neither did he acknowledge his brethren, nor knew his own children: for they have observed thy word, and kept thy covenant. ¹⁰They shall teach Jacob thy judgments, and Israel thy law: they *shall put incense before thee, and whole burnt sacrifice upon thine altar. [11] Bless, LORD, his substance, and accept the work of his hands; smite through the loins of them that rise against him, and of them that hate him, that they rise not again. [12] And of Benjamin he said, The beloved of the LORD shall dwell in safety by him; and the Lord shall cover him all the day long, and he shall dwell between his shoulders. [13] And of Joseph he said, Blessed of the LORD be his land, for the precious things of heaven, for the dew, and for the deep that coucheth beneath, [14] And for the precious fruits brought forth by the sun, and for the precious things put forth by the moon, [15] And for the chief things of the ancient mountains, and for the precious things of the lasting hills, [16] And for the precious things of the earth and fullness thereof, and for the good will of him that dwelt in the bush: let the blessing come upon the head of Joseph, and upon the top of the head of him that was separated from his brethren. [17] His glory is like the firstling of his bullock, and his horns are like the horns of unicorns: with them he shall push the people together to the ends of the earth: and they are the ten thousands of Ephraim, and they are the thousands of Manasseh. [18] And of Zebulun he said, Rejoice, Zebulun, in thy going out; and, Issachar, in thy tents. [19] They shall call the people unto the mountain; there they shall offer sacrifices of righteousness: for they shall suck of the abundance of the seas, and of treasures hid in the sand. [20] And of Gad he said, Blessed be he that enlargeth Gad: he dwelleth as a lion, and teareth the arm with the crown of the head. [21] And he provided the first part for himself, because there, in a portion of the lawgiver, was he seated; and he came with the heads of the people, he executed the justice of the LORD, and his judgments with Israel. [22] And of Dan he said, Dan is a lion's whelp: he shall leap from Bashan. [23] And of Naphtali he said, O Naphtali, satisfied with favour, and full with the blessing of the LORD: possess thou the west and the south. [24] And of Asher he said, Let Asher be blessed with children; let him be acceptable to his brethren, and let him dip his foot in oil. [25] Thy shoes shall be iron and brass; and as thy days, so shall thy strength be. [26] There is none like unto the God of Jeshurun, who rideth upon the heaven in thy help, and in his excellency on the sky. [27] The eternal God is thy refuge, and underneath are the everlasting arms: and he shall thrust out the enemy from before thee; and shall say, Destroy them. [28] Israel then shall dwell in safety alone: the fountain of Jacob shall be upon a land of corn and wine; also his heavens shall drop down dew. [29] Happy art thou, O Israel: who is like unto thee, O people saved by the LORD, the shield of thy help, and who is the sword of thy excellency! and thine enemies shall be found liars unto thee; and thou shalt tread upon their high places'*

If you look at Deuteronomy chapter 33, as Moses was blessing the children of Israel he never made any mention of Simeon. Simeon was not mentioned in the blessings of the children of Israel by the great prophet, Moses. In the same vein while other tribes were being blessed with all forms of inheritance, Levi had no physical inheritance. They were scattered all over Israel. For the sake of Moses, Aaron and Phineas (Aaron's grandson), Levi obtained God as their inheritance but there was no land inheritance for them. Simeon was squeezed into Judah and with time, was swallowed up by Judah. All because of that wicked action, that bitterness, that wickedness, they lost out! They were scattered. They were finished. No land inheritance, nothing!

See Joshua 19 (KJV)

'1 And the second lot came forth to Simeon, even for the tribe of the children of Simeon according to their families: and their inheritance was within the inheritance of the children of Judah. [2] And they had in their inheritance Beersheba, and Sheba, and Moladah, [3] And Hazarshual, and

Balah, and Azem, [4] And Eltolad, and Bethul, and Hormah, [5] And Ziklag, and Bethmarcaboth, and Hazarsusah, [6] And Bethlebaoth, and Sharuhen; thirteen cities and their villages: [7] Ain, Remmon, and Ether, and Ashan; four cities and their villages: [8] And all the villages that were round about these cities to Baalathbeer, Ramath of the south. This is the inheritance of the tribe of the children of Simeon according to their families. [9] Out of the portion of the children of Judah was the inheritance of the children of Simeon: for the part of the children of Judah was too much for them: therefore the children of Simeon had their inheritance within the inheritance of them'

Vengeance is mine, says the Lord. Leave vengeance unto God. Free yourself, empty yourself from that wicked spirit of vengefulness. It does no good. It has no good in it whatsoever, but self destruction. It destroys and makes nonsense of the carrier.

Simeon and Levi became tribes without land inheritance, no land for them, none whatsoever. They were scattered in Israel with no place to call their home. Their tribes were completely swallowed up by others. What a tragedy! And all because of a terrible spirit they harboured, the deadly unforgiving spirit. Generations unborn to these tribes had to suffer dislocations as a result of their patriarchs' unforgiving spirits.

The Breaking Out Of The Children Of Levi

Levi had his story changed along the line. This was because his children gave themselves to God and in doing that were recused from the curse that was on Levi. The

SIMEON AND LEVI, SONS OF JACOB

Lord chose Moses to be the one to lead His people, Israel, out of Egypt. Moses at his choice made a lot of excuses and complaints on why he is not the right candidate for the job. God insisted he was the one for the job. In order to take care of one his complaints, God appointed Aaron his brother as his mouthpiece. From a position of a mouth piece to Moses, God made Aaron the High Priest of Israel and all his male children priests of the Most High God. Aaron and his children became the keepers and were in charge of the Tabernacle and every ordinance therein.

God sensing the enormity of the work of the Tabernacle chose the tribe of Levi to work with the family of Aaron (also a Levite) in maintaining and taking care of the outward things pertaining to the Tabernacle and in leading the people of Israel in worship of the Lord Almighty. God had to in addition, choose the tribe of Levi and in choosing them, He replaced the firstborn that he appropriated to himself after the death of the firstborns of the Egyptians, He now replaced that with the appropriation of the tribe of Levi.

Some events happened as the children of Israel were on exodus from Egypt that led to the choice of the Levites as God's inheritance. They showed in different occasions that though their patriarch Levi failed his father Jacob, they on their own are ready to stand with God even when none else stands with them.

Exodus 32: 15 to 28 (KJV)

15 And Moses turned, and went down from the mount, and the two tables of the testimony were in his hand: the tables were written on both their sides; on the one side and on the other were they written. **16** And the tables were the work of God, and the writing was the writing of God, graven upon the tables. **17** And when Joshua heard the noise of the people as they shouted, he said unto Moses, There is a noise of war in the camp. **18** And he said, It is not the voice of them that shout for mastery, neither is it the voice of them that cry for being overcome: but the noise of them that sing do I hear. **19** And it came to pass, as soon as he came nigh unto the camp, that he saw the calf, and the dancing: and Moses' anger waxed hot, and he cast the tables out of his hands, and brake them beneath the mount. **20** And he took the calf which they had made, and burnt it in the fire, and ground it to powder, and strawed it upon the water, and made the children of Israel drink of it.

21 And Moses said unto Aaron, What did this people unto thee, that thou hast brought so great a sin upon them? **22** And Aaron said, Let not the anger of my lord wax hot: thou knowest the people, that they are set on mischief. **23** For they said unto me, Make us gods, which shall go before us: for as for this Moses, the man that brought us up out of the land of Egypt, we wot not what is become of him. **24** And I said unto them, Whosoever hath any gold, let them break it off. So they gave it me: then I cast it into the fire, and there came out this calf. **25** And when Moses saw that the people were naked; (for Aaron had made them naked unto their shame among their enemies: #1# **26** Then Moses stood in the gate of the camp, and said, Who is on the Lord's side? let him come unto me. And all the sons of Levi gathered themselves together unto him. **27** And he said unto them, Thus saith the Lord God of Israel, Put every man his sword by his side, and go in and out from gate to gate throughout the camp, and slay every man his brother, and every man his companion, and every man his neighbour. **28** And the children of Levi did *according to the word of Moses: and there fell of the people that day about three thousand men*

Numbers 3: 5 to 13 (KJV)

5 And the Lord spake unto Moses, saying, 6 Bring the tribe of Levi near, and present them before Aaron the priest, that they may minister unto him. 7 And they shall keep his charge, and the charge of the whole congregation before the tabernacle of the congregation, to do the service of the tabernacle. 8 And they shall keep all the instruments of the tabernacle of the congregation, and the charge of the children of Israel, to do the service of the tabernacle. 9 And thou shalt give the Levites unto Aaron and to his sons: they are wholly given unto him out of the children of Israel. 10 And thou shalt appoint Aaron and his sons, and they shall wait on their priest's office: and the stranger that cometh nigh shall be put to death. 11 And the Lord spake unto Moses, saying, 12 And I, behold, I have taken the Levites from among the children of Israel instead of all the firstborn that openeth the matrix among the children of Israel: therefore the Levites shall be mine; 13 Because all the firstborn are mine; for on the day that I smote all the firstborn in the land of Egypt I hallowed unto me all the firstborn in Israel, both man and beast: mine shall they be: I am the Lord.

Numbers 8: 5 to 19

The Cleansing of the Levites

5 And the Lord spake unto Moses, saying, 6 Take the Levites from among the children of Israel, and cleanse them. 7 And thus shalt thou do unto them, to cleanse them: Sprinkle water of purifying upon them, and let them shave all their flesh, and let them wash their clothes, and so make themselves clean. **8** Then let them take a young bullock with his meat offering, even fine flour mingled with oil, and another young bullock shalt thou take for a sin offering. **9** And thou shalt bring the Levites before the tabernacle of the congregation: and thou shalt gather the whole assembly of the children of Israel together: **10** And thou shalt bring the Levites before the Lord: and the children of Israel shall put their hands upon the Levites: **11** And Aaron shall offer the Levites before the Lord for an offering of the children of Israel, that they may execute the service of the Lord. **12** And the Levites shall lay their hands upon the heads of the bullocks: and thou shalt offer the one for a sin offering, and the other for a burnt offering, unto the Lord, to make an atonement for the Levites. **13** And thou shalt set the Levites before Aaron, and before his sons, and offer them for an offering unto the Lord. **14** Thus shalt thou separate the Levites from among the children of Israel: and the Levites shall be mine. **15** And after that shall the Levites go in to do the service of the tabernacle of the congregation: and thou shalt cleanse them, and offer them for an offering. **16** For they are wholly given unto me from among the children of Israel; instead of such as open every womb, even instead of the firstborn of all the children of Israel, have I taken them unto me. **17** For all the firstborn of the children of Israel are mine, both man and beast: on the day that I smote every firstborn in the land of Egypt I sanctified them for myself. **18** And I have taken the Levites for all the firstborn of the children of Israel. **19** And I have given the Levites as a gift to Aaron and to his sons from among the children of Israel, to do the service of the children of Israel in the tabernacle of the congregation, and to make an atonement for the children of Israel: that there be no plague among the children of Israel, when the children of Israel come nigh unto the sanctuary.

Deuteronomy 10: 8 to 9 (KJV)

SIMEON AND LEVI, SONS OF JACOB

8 At that time the Lord separated the tribe of Levi, to bear the ark of the covenant of the Lord, to stand before the Lord to minister unto him, and to bless in his name, unto this day. 9 Wherefore Levi hath no part nor inheritance with his brethren; the Lord is his inheritance, according as the Lord thy God promised him.

God appropriated the Levites to join hands with the family of Aaron in doing the work of the sanctuary. By that appropriation the Levite came into something much bigger than was desired for him by his father Jacob. God chose Levi as a special inheritance and then turned around and gave Himself to the Levites as their inheritance, even though they were dispossessed by their patriarch, Jacob, God gave them a better inheritance. And so God said, I will be your inheritance, yes, you will not inherit any land as a tribe but I would be your inheritance. Of course, God Being their inheritance became far superior to inheriting land. The lineage, the tribe of Levi became the tribe for the priests, became the tribe of those that will do the work of the sanctuary, the tribe to carry the Ark, the tribe that will take hold of everything that pertains to the place of worship of God. That of course, is far superior to inheriting only land.

This is also a very big lesson for all of us. Instead of giving life to generational curse or generation bitterness, you can turn the clock around by breaking the generational bitterness and curse by accepting God in His totality. This you can do by making God your inheritance and allowing God to make you His own inheritance. Surely, the end result will become far better and superior to living a life of unforgiveness that you acquired through generations past.

Levi's case became a different issue altogether, while Simeon suffered a total annihilation, Levi went on and on, that to this day, the priests, the rabbis and those in responsible positions in the Jewish religion are sons of Aaron and the Levites. That's where God has called us today as His children, Levites, people that will stand in the gap, people that will stand to do the work of the sanctuary, and people that God can depend on, those that have God as their inheritance. Instead of wallowing and living a life of unforgiveness, why not turn around and give yourself to Christ as a Levite to do the work of the sanctuary with all your heart and all your being and God will not only be your inheritance, you will also become God's inheritance.

May The Lord help us and bring us into this place of the beautifulness of God. Praise the Lord. Amen.

Let us learn from these. All these stories about unforgiveness and the aftermaths are for our learning and deliverance. Resentment destroys, it has nothing good in it. It only has destruction as its fruit. It destroys, it doesn't pay any blissful dividend at all. That's why we should pray God to bless us with a large heart that forgives, that frees people and frees ourselves. When you have a heart that forgives, you live a free life, you will be free and your system will become free to enjoy life.

But when your heart is filled with the unforgiving spirit, you will age quickly and your life will be in torment because you will be filled with thoughts of vengeance and what you would do to avenge. The desire to avenge would eat you up. Even if you succeed in avenging (like Simeon and Levi did) the same action which you avenged would become the seed that would lead to your own destruction.

Why then do we kill ourselves by carrying this very heavy load of vengefulness that will eventually destroy us? Free yourself. Loosen your heart. Set yourself free from this wickedness, this cruelty. Jacob said, "Cursed be this cruelty of yours, this anger. Cursed be it because it's not of God, it does not in any way yield the righteousness of God rather it yields the wickedness of the devil. Free your heart, free your spirit, and free your being from every form of resentment so that you may enjoy the life God has purposed for you. Amen.

CHAPTER 4
KORAH THE LEVITE
Thought of Himself More Highly Than Others

Numbers 16: 1 - 40 (KJV)

16 Now Korah, the son of Izhar, the son of Kohath, the son of Levi, and Dathan and Abiram, the sons of Eliab, and On, the son of Peleth, sons of Reuben, took men: [2] And they rose up before Moses, with certain of the children of Israel, two hundred and fifty princes of the assembly, famous in the congregation, men of renown: [3] And they gathered themselves together against Moses and against Aaron, and said unto them, Ye take too much upon you, seeing all the congregation are holy, every one of them, and the LORD is among them: wherefore then lift ye up yourselves above the congregation of the LORD? [4] And when Moses heard it, he fell upon his face: [5] And he spake unto Korah and unto all his company, saying, Even tomorrow the LORD will shew who are his, and who is holy; and will cause him to come near unto him: even him whom he hath chosen will he cause to come near unto him. [6] This do; Take you censers, Korah, and all his company; [7] And put fire therein, and put incense in them before the LORD tomorrow: and it shall be that the man whom the LORD doth choose, he shall be holy: ye take too much upon you, ye sons of Levi. [8] And Moses said unto Korah, Hear, I pray you, ye sons of Levi: [9] Seemeth it but a small thing unto you, that the God of Israel hath separated you from the congregation of Israel, to bring you near to himself to do the service of the tabernacle of the LORD, and to stand before the congregation to minister unto them? [10] And he hath brought thee near to him, and all thy brethren the sons of Levi with thee: and seek ye the priesthood also? [11] For which cause both thou and all thy company are gathered together against the LORD: and what is Aaron, that

36

ye murmur against him? [12] And Moses sent to call Dathan and Abiram, the sons of Eliab: which said, We will not come up: [13] Is it a small thing that thou hast brought us up out of a land that floweth with milk and honey, to kill us in the wilderness, except thou make thyself altogether a prince over us? [14] Moreover thou hast not brought us into a land that floweth with milk and honey, or given us inheritance of fields and vineyards: wilt thou put out the eyes of these men? we will not come up. [15] And Moses was very wroth, and said unto the LORD, Respect not thou their offering: I have not taken one ass from them, neither have I hurt one of them. [16] And Moses said unto Korah, Be thou and all thy company before the LORD, thou, and they, and Aaron, tomorrow: [17] And take every man his censer, and put incense in them, and bring ye before the LORD every man his censer, two hundred and fifty censers; thou also, and Aaron, each of you his censer. [18] And they took every man his censer, and put fire in them, and laid incense thereon, and stood in the door of the tabernacle of the congregation with Moses and Aaron. [19] And Korah gathered all the congregation against them unto the door of the tabernacle of the congregation: and the glory of the LORD appeared unto all the congregation. [20] And the LORD spake unto Moses and unto Aaron, saying, [21] Separate yourselves from among this congregation, that I may consume them in a moment. [22] And they fell upon their faces, and said, O God, the God of the spirits of all flesh, shall one man sin, and wilt thou be wroth with all the congregation? [23] And the LORD spake unto Moses, saying, [24] Speak unto the congregation, saying, Get you up from about the tabernacle of Korah, Dathan, and Abiram. [25] And Moses rose up and went unto Dathan and Abiram; and the elders of Israel followed him. [26] And he spake unto the congregation, saying, Depart, I pray you, from the tents of these wicked men, and touch nothing of theirs, lest ye be consumed in all their sins. [27] So they gat up from the tabernacle of Korah, Dathan, and Abiram, on every side: and Dathan and Abiram came out, and stood in the door of their tents, and their wives, and their sons, and their little children. ²⁸ And Moses said, Hereby ye shall know that the LORD hath sent me to do all these works; for I have not done them of mine own mind. ²⁹ If these men die the common death of all men, or if they be visited after the visitation of all men; then the LORD hath not sent me. ³⁰ But if the LORD make a new thing, and the earth open her mouth, and swallow them up, with all that appertain unto them, and they go down quick into the pit; then ye shall understand that these men have provoked the LORD. ³¹ And it came to pass, as he had made an end of speaking all these words, that the ground clave asunder that was under them: ³² And the earth opened her mouth, and swallowed them up, and their houses, and all the men that appertained unto Korah, and all their goods. ³³ They, and all that appertained to them, went down alive into the pit, and the earth closed upon them: and they perished from among the congregation. ³⁴ And all Israel that were round about them fled at the cry of them: for they said, Lest the earth swallow us up also. ³⁵ And there came out a fire from the LORD, and consumed the two hundred and fifty men that offered incense. ³⁶ And the LORD spake unto Moses, saying, ³⁷ Speak unto Eleazar the son of Aaron the priest, that he take up the censers out of the burning, and scatter thou the fire yonder; for they are hallowed. ³⁸ The censers of these sinners against their own souls, let them make them broad plates for a covering of the altar: for they offered them before the LORD, therefore they are hallowed: and they shall be a sign unto the children of Israel. ³⁹ And Eleazar the priest took the brasen censers, wherewith they that were burnt had offered; and they were made broad plates for a covering of the altar: ⁴⁰ To be a memorial unto the children of Israel, that no stranger, which is not of the seed of Aaron, come near to offer incense before the LORD; that he be not as Korah, and as his company: as the LORD said to him by the hand of Moses.

KORAH THE LEVITE

The man, Korah, was a great son of Israel who allowed bitterness and an unforgiving spirit rooted in jealousy and envy to lead to his destruction. Let us firstly look at his lineage. Korah was the son of Izhar, the son of Kohath, the son of Levi, the son of Jacob. Aaron, on the other hand, was the son of Amram, the son of Kohath, the son of Levi, the son of Jacob. In other words, Korah and Aaron and Moses were from the same Kohath lineage. Korah was a cousin to Aaron and Moses. They did not only come from the same tribe of Levi, they all came from the sub-tribe of Kohath. Aaron and Korah must have known each other from childhood since Moses grew up in the house of Pharaoh during his early years as a Prince of Egypt. So Korah and Aaron must have known themselves very much; most probably, they were peers. Korah may have discovered a lot of weaknesses in Aaron: his inabilities, his dullness and a lot of other things about Aaron that made him incapable of being a good and wonderful leader. Those were some of the things he saw that formed his perception of Aaron. He saw him as a weakling with little or no leadership traits.

Aaron expounded this further with the way he handled the demands of the children of Israel when Moses spent a long time on the mountain communing with God. Aaron displayed weak character when he succumbed to the pressures put on him by the children of Israel who demanded that he make a golden calf for them. That, to a great extent, showed how Aaron lacked some leadership traits and laid bare his weakness.

I tend to think that Korah must have observed all these events as they played out in Aaron's life, in addition to all he knew about him from their childhood days; being a cousin and probable playmate. He just could not see himself, an intelligent man full of grace and vigour, endowed with leadership traits and all, submit to this weakling. You can see that his family became songwriters, psalmists and prophets – Prophet Samuel was from his lineage – and excellent craftsmen.

It was therefore difficult for him to understand how Aaron could be the High Priest with all his frailties and inabilities while he, being full of life, powerful, intelligent, arrogant and full of himself would be subjected to carrying the holy things and excluded from the priesthood not to talk of the high priesthood. That was a very big blow on him and on his ego and on all that he stood for. He could not take it; he just couldn't take it.

The Ways Of God Are Beyond Man's Understanding

Korah could not understand how God could choose somebody like Aaron with all his inabilities and bypass a *solid* man of high intelligence as he. He did not understand the mechanisms of God. It was difficult for him to appreciate that God does not see as man sees. God does not choose as man chooses. This aspect of God manifested itself plainly when God sent Samuel to the house of Jesse to anoint a new king for Israel after the failure of King Saul to live and rule in obedience to God's commands.

KORAH THE LEVITE

See 1st Samuel Chapter 16 verses 1 to 13:

1 Samuel 16 (KJV)

1 And the LORD said unto Samuel, How long wilt thou mourn for Saul, seeing I have rejected him from reigning over Israel? fill thine horn with oil, and go, I will send thee to Jesse the Bethlehemite: for I have provided me a king among his sons. ² And Samuel said, How can I go? If Saul hear it, he will kill me. And the LORD said, Take an heifer with thee, and say, I am come to sacrifice to the LORD. ³ And call Jesse to the sacrifice, and I will shew thee what thou shalt do: and thou shalt anoint unto me him whom I name unto thee. ⁴ And Samuel did that which the LORD spake, and came to Bethlehem. And the elders of the town trembled at his coming, and said, Comest thou peaceably? ⁵ And he said, Peaceably: I am come to sacrifice unto the LORD: sanctify yourselves, and come with me to the sacrifice. And he sanctified Jesse and his sons, and called them to the sacrifice. ⁶ And it came to pass, when they were come, that he looked on Eliab, and said, Surely the LORD's anointed is before him. ⁷ But the LORD said unto Samuel, Look not on his countenance, or on the height of his stature; because I have refused him: for the LORD seeth not as man seeth; for man looketh on the outward appearance, but the LORD looketh on the heart. ⁸ Then Jesse called Abinadab, and made him pass before Samuel. And he said, Neither hath the LORD chosen this. ⁹ Then Jesse made Shammah to pass by. And he said, Neither hath the LORD chosen this. ¹⁰ Again, Jesse made seven of his sons to pass before Samuel. And Samuel said unto Jesse, The LORD hath not chosen these. ¹¹ And Samuel said unto Jesse, Are here all thy children? And he said, There remaineth yet the youngest, and, behold, he keepeth the sheep. And Samuel said unto Jesse, Send and fetch him: for we will not sit down till he come hither. ¹² And he sent, and brought him in. Now he was ruddy, and withal of a beautiful countenance, and goodly to

look to. And the LORD said, Arise, anoint him: for this is he.
¹³ Then Samuel took the horn of oil, and anointed him in the
midst of his brethren: and the Spirit of the LORD came upon
David from that day forward. So Samuel rose up, and went
to Ramah.

As far as Samuel was concerned, the brothers of David were kingly men by their statures; everything about them from man's perspective was intact but God said, "No! None of them is the person I want". But one ruddy young man who lived all his life in the bush tending sheep and cattle was the one that God chose.

God looks beyond what the eyes of man see. He looks beyond what is attractive to man. Korah could not bring himself to appreciate God's choice but out of envy and jealousy, he gathered some people who were loyal to him to fight Moses and dethrone Aaron. It was a complete mess.

That is what resentment, bitterness, envy and jealousy can breed. This is so similar to the case of Cain. Cain was very angry as to why God chose to accept the sacrifice of Abel but rejected his. Cain killed Abel with the hope that God would change his decision and accept his sacrifice.

In both cases, the objects of Cain and Korah's anger and bitterness, Abel and Aaron, were not privy neither were they participants in God's decision concerning them. The criteria for God's choice were solely His without any human input. It was therefore very sad that men who were chosen as a result of God's wisdom became recipients of adverse hatred and bitterness.

The Sad End Of Korah

In the sight of Korah, Aaron was not qualified to be the High Priest. "Why should it be Aaron," he contemplated, "when there were so many other better-qualified men from his tribe and sub tribe?" He reasoned from the perspective of a man and so he conspired against Moses and Aaron with two hundred and fifty loyal and exceptional princes of Israel who agreed with him that Aaron was not fit to serve in the office of the High Priest. What they failed to understand was that they were not fighting against Aaron and Moses but against God's decision.

It was a terrible thing; a result of uncontrolled jealousy and envy which eventually led to bitterness and resentment. It led to the rejection of God's choice and direct order while Korah was more interested in instituting his own choice and order and forcing it on others. He lured many people who believed in his abilities, strength and administrative prowess and together, they said, "No! Korah should be a better leader and high priest. They went as far as accepting the challenge to prove that God was in support of their disobedience and evil.

What was the consequence of this act? The earth opened up and swallowed them all, including all family members who supported their rebellion. However, some of Korah's children refused to stand one with him in rejecting God's orders hence; they were saved from the calamity that befell those who were bold enough to challenge God.

In response to the question, "Who were the sons of Korah in the Old Testament?" the owners of the website-GotQuestions.org[2] gave an impressive answer. So, with their permission, the answer is published below:

"The story of the sons of Korah in the Old Testament is truly a tale of two fathers and two destinies. The story begins with the Israelites of Moses' time as they journeyed through the wilderness just after leaving Egypt. In Numbers 3, God set aside the Levites, out of the tribes of Israel, for full time service to Him. They were ordained to take care of the tabernacle and all of its implements, as well as the Ark of the Covenant. Only the descendants of Aaron, however, were allowed to serve as priests.

The three sons of Levi were Gershon, Merari, and Kohath. The Gershonites were responsible for the care of the tabernacle and tent, its coverings, the curtain at the entrance to the tent of meeting, the curtains of the courtyard, the curtain at the entrance to the courtyard surrounding the tabernacle and altar, and the ropes—and everything related to their use. The Merarites were appointed to take care of the frames of the tabernacle, its crossbars, posts, bases, all its equipment, and everything related to their use, as well as the posts of the surrounding courtyard with their bases, tent pegs, and ropes. The Kohathites were responsible for the care of the sanctuary. They were responsible for the care of the ark, the table, the lamp stand, the altars, the articles of the sanctuary used in ministering, the curtain, and everything related to their use. They were under the direct supervision of Eleazar, son of Aaron.

Unlike the Gershonites and the Merarites, who were allowed to transport the items under their care on carts, the Kohathites had to carry their items, the holy things of the tabernacle, on their shoulders. They had the arduous burden of transporting these items from place to place as the camp moved, but they were not allowed to actually touch the items or they would die. The priests had to wrap the sacred objects in special coverings before they were transported (Numbers 4:15). Many of the Kohathites began to disdain this task and to covet the role of the priests.

Korah was the grandson of Kohath, and he began to run with another group of Reubenite malcontents, namely, Dathan and Abiram, sons of Eliab, and On, son of Peleth. In pride, they roused a group of 250 men together to challenge the right of Moses and Aaron to the priesthood (Numbers 16). Moses summoned the rebellious men to stand before God and burn incense. God warned Moses to let the assembly know to get away from Korah, Dathan, and Abiram, their households, and the other rebels. Then a remarkable and terrifying event happened.

"Moses said, 'This is how you will know that the LORD has sent me to do all these things and that it was not my idea: If these men die a natural death and suffer the fate of all mankind, then the LORD has not sent me. But if the LORD brings about something totally new, and the earth opens its mouth and swallows them, with everything that belongs to them, and they go down alive into the realm of the dead, then you will know that these men have treated the LORD with contempt.' As soon as he finished saying all this, the ground under them split apart and the earth opened its mouth and swallowed them and their households, and all those associated with Korah, together with their possessions. They went down alive into the realm of the dead, with everything they owned; the earth closed over them, and they perished and were gone from the community. At their cries, all the Israelites around them fled, shouting, 'The earth is going to swallow us too!' And fire came out from the LORD and consumed the 250 men who were offering the incense" (Numbers 16:28–35).

Although this clearly marked the end of Korah, we discover that Korah's sons, perhaps too young to understand their father's uprising or maybe too cognizant of God's authority to join in the revolt, were spared (Numbers 26:9–11). God judged those who turned against Him in active rebellion and purified His people, but He still had a purpose and plan for even the line of Korah. After seven successive generations, the prophet Samuel arose from the line of Korah, the genealogy of which is recorded in 1 Chronicles 6:31–38, 1 Chronicles 38, and 1 Samuel 1:1, 20. The Korahites became doorkeepers and custodians for the tabernacle (1 Chronicles 9:19–21; 1 Chronicles 2.) One group of Korahites (1 Chronicles 12:6) joined King David in various military exploits and won the reputation of being expert warriors. However, the most remarkable thing to note about the sons of Korah is that during the time of King David, they became the great leaders in choral and orchestral music in the tabernacle. Heman the Korahite had a place of great importance as a singer, along with Asaph (a Gershonite) and Ethan or Jeduthan (a Merarite). These individuals played an important role in the thanksgiving services and pageantry when the Ark of the Covenant was brought to Jerusalem. David formed an elaborate organisation for song, instrumental music, and prophesying through these men.

Of all of the psalms in the Bible, eleven are attributed to the sons of Korah. These beautiful psalms express a spirit of great gratitude and humility to an awesome, mighty God. They express a longing for God and deep devotion. These poetic songs include Psalms 42—50, 62, and 72—85. Psalm 42:1 contains the beautiful line, "As the deer pants for flowing streams, so pants my soul for you,

O God." Psalm 84:1 states, "How lovely is your dwelling place, O God." Psalm 46:1–3 conveys the powerful message, "God is our refuge and strength, an ever-present help in trouble. Therefore we will not fear, though the earth give way and the mountains fall into the heart of the sea, though its waters roar and foam and the mountains quake with their surging."

One wonders if the poet who penned these lyrics was remembering his ignoble beginnings, his distant ancestor who perished in an earthquake for his pride and rebellion. Perhaps it was that reflection that prompted the following words of the same psalm: "He says, 'Be still, and know that I am God; I will be exalted among the nations, I will be exalted in the earth'" (Psalm 46:10). For each of us, our own songs of renewed purpose and redemption should flow out of a heart of humility as we remember the fallen state from which He raised us and the redemption that we experience through His grace. This was certainly the case for the sons of Korah"

Save Your Life, Do Not Challenge God's Choice

He was destroyed because he was blinded by jealousy which bred resentment against a man that did nothing to him. Aaron may have had lots of visible weaknesses, nonetheless, God still chose him with his disability and weaknesses.

KORAH THE LEVITE

It is God that chooses. His criteria may not be made known to us but we must not rebel against God's choice. It is up to God and Him alone; it is all about God. Everything that has to do with God's choice is all about God; He owes no one any apologies for choosing anyone into any position. It's God's business. So, your jealousy or envy over his choice is a sure road to ultimate destruction.

All we need do is to accept and submit to God's choice for He only knows why He made the choice and He has no explanation whatsoever to make to us. This was what was wrong with Korah: he rebelled against God's choice and His anointed and God had to show him that it is not man who makes choices for Him; God chooses for himself.

I don't know who you are bearing some grudges against because of the position God has placed him in. You might have been planning all sorts of evil to bring him down but my candid advice to you is that the way you are going is a way that leads to destruction. You had better make a U-Turn, accept God's choice and submit to Him.

Know that if He appoints a man to be a head over you, and you submit to that man, invariably, you are submitting to God. So you had better do the right thing for the sake of your life and the lives of all those with you. But if you desire to be like Korah, then you are leading yourself and all those following you to destruction. What awaits you and all who connive with you is destruction. Let God's choice stand and save your life by accepting the choice of God. Amen.

ABIMELECH, GIDEON'S SON
Nursed Hurts over Years while Biding Time

We will begin by looking at Judges Chapter 8 versus 30 and 31.

> "30 And Gideon had threescore and ten sons of his body begotten: for he had many wives. 31 And his concubine that was in Shechem, she also bare him a son, whose name he called Abimelech." (KJV)

From the scriptures, we see that Gideon had 70 sons from his wives. Apart from the sons from his wives, he also had a concubine in Shechem. This concubine bore him a son called Abimelech.

Abimelech was not a legitimate son because he was born of a concubine of Gideon. To some extent, from events that followed later, one could conveniently say that Abimelech had grudges in his heart against his brothers. This was because they were legitimate sons of Gideon and were treated as such while he, on the other hand, was probably treated in a completely different way.

Abimelech bore this grudge, and in chapter 9 of Judges, we see the fruits of this grudge and his unforgiveness. He bore an unforgiving spirit in him against the 70 legitimate sons, and because this wicked spirit possessed him, he bided time to take revenge for the way he had been maltreated.

Plan To Avenge His Hurt

At the death of Gideon, Abimelech went to his mother's people, the people of Shechem, and convinced them to be partakers of his plan to express his unforgiving spirit. He convinced them that he was one of them since his mother was from Shechem.

Judges Chapter 9

"1 And Abimelech the son of Jerubbaal went to Shechem unto his mother's brethren, and communed with them, and with all the family of the house of his mother's father, saying, ²Speak, I pray you, in the ears of all the men of Shechem, Whether is better for you, either that all the sons of Jerubbaal, which are threescore and ten persons, reign over you, or that one reign over you? Remember also that I am your bone and your flesh. ³And his mother's brethren spake of him in the ears of all the men of Shechem all these words: and their hearts inclined to follow Abimelech; for they said, He is our brother. ⁴And they gave him threescore and ten pieces of silver out of the house of Baalberith, wherewith Abimelech hired vain and light persons, which followed him. ⁵And he went unto his father's house at Ophrah, and slew his brethren the sons of Jerubbaal, being threescore and ten persons, upon one stone: notwithstanding yet Jotham the youngest son of Jerubbaal was left; for he hid himself. ⁶And all the men of Shechem gathered together, and all the house of Millo, and went, and made Abimelech king, by the plain of the pillar that was in Shechem."(KJV)

Abimelech conspired with them and slaughtered the seventy sons of Gideon, save one that escaped from them. We can see a trend here. A trend that if you nurse something in your heart that is not right, it can lead to a terrible situation in the future. He nursed evil in his heart because he felt he was not treated rightly and then, he avenged his evil desire on his brothers. And at the death of his father, he connived with his mother's people to kill his seventy step-brothers.

The Result Of His Dastardly Action

Now let's look at what followed after this. After this vengeance, what followed? He ruled over Israel from Shechem for three years and after that the very people of Schechem who connived and conspired with him to destroy the house of Gideon planned to destroy him. Gideon ruled over Israel and brought peace in Israel, defeated the Philistine's and lived a life that at a point, he refused to be made king but rather told them that God is only the King that Israel should have.

Judges Chapter 9

> "²² When Abimelech had reigned three years over Israel, ²³ Then God sent an evil spirit between Abimelech and the men of Shechem; and the men of Shechem dealt treacherously with Abimelech: ²⁴ That the cruelty done to the threescore and ten sons of Jerubbaal might come, and their blood be laid upon Abimelech their brother, which slew them; and upon the men of Shechem, which aided him in the killing of his brethren. ²⁵ And the men of Shechem set liers in wait for him in the top of the mountains, and they robbed all that came along that way by them: and it was told Abimelech." (KJV)

The people of Shechem had conspired with Abimelech

and destroyed the house of Gideon. Then, this same people, after a number of years, conspired to destroy him.

You see, like I have mentioned previously, this thing called unforgiveness leads to a dead end, a dead end that destroys the one who has refused to forgive.

Abimelech got to the point where even the people that helped him fulfil his desire for vengeance, arising from his unforgiving spirit, were now the same people that turned around and said he was no good. And for their turn around, he made war against them and in the course of the war, he met his end.

Judges Chapter 9

> "34 And Abimelech rose up, and all the people that were with him, by night, and they laid wait against Shechem in four companies.
> 44 And Abimelech, and the company that was with him, rushed forward, and stood in the entering of the gate of the city: and the two other companies ran upon all the people that were in the fields, and slew them. 45 And Abimelech fought against the city all that day; and he took the city, and slew the people that was therein, and beat down the city, and sowed it with salt. 46 And when all the men of the tower of Shechem heard that, they entered into an hold of the house of the god Berith. 47 And it was told Abimelech, that all the men of the tower of Shechem were gathered together. 48 And Abimelech gat him up to mount Zalmon, he and all the people that were with him; and Abimelech took an axe in his hand, and cut down a bough from the trees, and took it, and

laid it on his shoulder, and said unto the people that were with him, What ye have seen me do, make haste, and do as I have done. [49] And all the people likewise cut down every man his bough, and followed Abimelech, and put them to the hold, and set the hold on fire upon them; so that all the men of the tower of Shechem died also, about a thousand men and women. [50] Then went Abimelech to Thebez, and encamped against Thebez, and took it. [51] But there was a strong tower within the city, and thither fled all the men and women, and all they of the city, and shut it to them, and gat them up to the top of the tower. [52] And Abimelech came unto the tower, and fought against it, and went hard unto the door of the tower to burn it with fire. [53] And a certain woman cast a piece of a millstone upon Abimelech's head, and all to break his skull. [54] Then he called hastily unto the young man his armour bearer, and said unto him, Draw thy sword, and slay me, that men say not of me, A women slew him. And his young man thrust him through, and he died."(KJV)

His end came after he had destroyed many cities in Shechem. As he went after another city to destroy it, he met his end. That is the way it always happens, with this thing called unforgiveness.

When the men of Israel saw that Abimelech was dead, they departed every man unto his place. Judges chapter 9 verse 56 reads:

*"**God rendered the wickedness of Abimelech which he did unto his father in slaying his seventy brethren. And all the evil of the men of Shechem, did God render upon their heads and upon them came the curse of Jotham the son of Gideon.***

That was the end of Abimelech; killed by a woman, who cast a stone upon his head and smashed his skull, all because of resentment. Probably, he had been constantly taunted as the son of a concubine and this may have made him bear grudges which later grew into resentment and made him bide his time to avenge the ills he believed were done to him.

The Reward Of His Collaborators

He did not just carry out his act of revenge alone, but gathered his mother's people to do it with him, at a great cost to the house of Gideon. From this, you can see that a vengeful spirit tends to come around and eat up its bearer. That is what happened to Abimelech and the people of Shechem. It turned around, went full circle and came back on them, he was killed by the stone thrown by a woman.

Before his destruction, he was also the instrument used by the same wicked spirit to destroy the people of Shechem- his collaborators and co-conspirators. The one that refuses to forgive usually gets destroyed by the events that proceed out of that attitude.

That is why we have to, at all times, free our spirits, free our beings and free ourselves from this wicked spirit of unforgiveness.

This spirit is a destroyer and a spirit of destruction. It

destroys one completely and brings them to nothingness. It is not a spirit that you should welcome in any form, in any way and in any measure. It should not be welcomed because in its fullness, it destroys the bearer. Welcoming the unforgiving spirit is tantamount to welcoming destruction for your life.

May the Lord save us. Amen and Amen!

CHAPTER 6

SAUL, FIRST KING OF ISRAEL
Had an Unforgiving Spirit Born of Misplaced Aggression

1 Samuel 8 (KJV)

And it came to pass, when Samuel was old, that he made his sons judges over Israel. 2 Now the name of his firstborn was Joel; and the name of his second, Abiah: they were judges in Beersheba. 3 And his sons walked not in his ways, but turned aside after lucre, and took bribes, and perverted judgment.

4 Then all the elders of Israel gathered themselves together, and came to Samuel unto Ramah, 5 And said unto him, Behold, thou art old, and thy sons walk not in thy ways: now make us a king to judge us like all the nations. 6 But the thing displeased Samuel, when they said, Give us a king to judge us. And Samuel prayed unto the Lord. 7 And the Lord said unto Samuel, Hearken unto the voice of the people in all that they say unto thee: for they have not rejected thee, but they have rejected me, that I should not reign over them. 8 According to all the works which they have done since the day that I brought them up out of Egypt even unto this day, wherewith they have forsaken me, and served other gods, so do they also unto thee. 9 Now therefore hearken unto their voice: howbeit yet protest solemnly unto them, and shew them the manner of the king that shall reign over them. 10 And Samuel told all the words of the Lord unto the people that asked of him a king. 11 And he said, This will be the manner of the king that shall reign over you: He will take your sons, and appoint them for himself, for his chariots, and to be his horsemen; and some shall run before his chariots. 12 And he will appoint him captains over thousands, and captains over fifties; and will set them to ear his ground, and to reap his harvest, and to make his instruments of war, and instruments of his chariots. 13 And he will take your daughters to be confectionaries, and to be cooks, and to be bakers. 14 And he will take your fields, and your vineyards, and your oliveyards, even the best of them, and give them to his servants. 15 And he will take the tenth of your seed, and of your vineyards, and give to his officers, and to his servants. 16 And he will take your menservants, and your maidservants, and your goodliest young men, and your asses, and put them to his work. 17 He will take the tenth of your sheep: and ye shall be his servants. 18 And ye shall cry out in that day because of your king which ye shall have chosen you; and the Lord will not hear you in that day. 19 Nevertheless the people refused to obey the voice of Samuel; and they said, Nay; but we will have a king over us; 20 That we also may be like all the nations; and that our king may judge us, and go out before us, and fight our battles. 21 And Samuel heard all the words of the people, and he rehearsed them in the ears of the Lord. 22 And the Lord said to Samuel, Hearken unto their voice, and make them a king. And Samuel said unto the men of Israel, Go ye every man unto his city.

1 Samuel 10 (KJV)

1 Then Samuel took a vial of oil, and poured it upon his head, and kissed him, and said, Is it not because the Lord hath anointed thee to be captain over his inheritance? 2 When thou art departed from me today, then thou shalt find two men by Rachel's sepulchre in the border of Benjamin at Zelzah; and they will say unto thee, The asses which thou wentest to seek are found: and, lo, thy father hath left the care of the asses, and sorroweth for you, saying, What shall I do for my son? 3 Then shalt thou go on forward from thence, and thou shalt come to the plain of Tabor, and there shall meet thee three men going up to God to Bethel, one

carrying three kids, and another carrying three loaves of bread, and another carrying a bottle of wine: 4 And they will salute thee, and give thee two loaves of bread; which thou shalt receive of their hands. 5 After that thou shalt come to the hill of God, where is the garrison of the Philistines: and it shall come to pass, when thou art come thither to the city, that thou shalt meet a company of prophets coming down from the high place with a psaltery, and a tabret, and a pipe, and a harp, before them; and they shall prophesy: 6 And the Spirit of the Lord will come upon thee, and thou shalt prophesy with them, and shalt be turned into another man. 7 And let it be, when these signs are come unto thee, that thou do as occasion serve thee; for God is with thee. 8 And thou shalt go down before me to Gilgal; and, behold, I will come down unto thee, to offer burnt offerings, and to sacrifice sacrifices of peace offerings: seven days shalt thou tarry, till I come to thee, and shew thee what thou shalt do. 9 And it was so, that when he had turned his back to go from Samuel, God gave him another heart: and all those signs came to pass that day. 10 And when they came thither to the hill, behold, a company of prophets met him; and the Spirit of God came upon him, and he prophesied among them. 11 And it came to pass, when all that knew him beforetime saw that, behold, he prophesied among the prophets, then the people said one to another, What is this that is come unto the son of Kish? Is Saul also among the prophets? 12 And one of the same place answered and said, But who is their father? Therefore it became a proverb, Is Saul also among the prophets? 13 And when he had made an end of prophesying, he came to the high place. 14 And Saul's uncle said unto him and to his servant, Whither went ye? And he said, To seek the asses: and when we saw that they were nowhere, we came to Samuel. 15 And Saul's uncle said, Tell me, I pray thee, what Samuel said unto you. 16 And Saul said unto his uncle, He told us plainly that the asses were found. But of the matter of the kingdom, whereof Samuel spake, he told him not. 17 And Samuel called the people together unto the Lord to Mizpeh; 18 And said unto the children of Israel, Thus saith the Lord God of Israel, I brought up Israel out of Egypt, and delivered you out of the hand of the Egyptians, and out of the hand of all kingdoms, and of them that oppressed you: 19 And ye have this day rejected your God, who himself saved you out of all your adversities and your tribulations; and ye have said unto him, Nay, but set a king over us. Now therefore present yourselves before the Lord by your tribes, and by your thousands. 20 And when Samuel had caused all the tribes of Israel to come near, the tribe of Benjamin was taken. 21 When he had caused the tribe of Benjamin to come near by their families, the family of Matri was taken, and Saul the son of Kish was taken: and when they sought him, he could not be found. 22 Therefore they enquired of the Lord further, if the man should yet come thither. And the Lord answered, Behold, he hath hid himself among the stuff. 23 And they ran and fetched him thence: and when he stood among the people, he was higher than any of the people from his shoulders and upward. 24 And Samuel said to all the people, See ye him whom the Lord hath chosen, that there is none like him among all the people? And all the people shouted, and said, God save the king. 25 Then Samuel told the people the manner of the kingdom, and wrote it in a book, and laid it up before the Lord. And Samuel sent all the people away, every man to his house. 26 And Saul also went home to Gibeah; and there went with him a band of men, whose hearts God had touched. 27 But the children of Belial said, How shall this man save us? And they despised him, and brought him no presents. But he held his peace.

1 Samuel 15 (KJV)

Saul's Disobedience and Rejection

15 Samuel also said unto Saul, The Lord sent me to anoint thee to be king over his people, over Israel: now therefore hearken thou unto the voice of the words of the Lord. **2** Thus saith the Lord of hosts, I remember that which Amalek did to Israel, how he laid wait for him in the way, when he came up from Egypt. **3** Now go and smite Amalek, and utterly destroy all that they have, and spare them not; but slay both man and woman, infant and suckling, ox and sheep, camel and ass. **4** And Saul gathered the people together, and numbered them in Telaim, two hundred thousand footmen, and ten thousand men of Judah. **5** And Saul came to a city of Amalek, and laid wait in the valley. **6** And Saul said unto the Kenites, Go, depart, get you down from among the Amalekites, lest I destroy you with them: for ye shewed kindness to all the children of Israel, when they came up out of Egypt. So the Kenites departed from among the Amalekites. **7** And Saul smote the Amalekites from Havilah until thou comest to Shur, that is over against Egypt. **8** And he took Agag the king of the Amalekites alive, and utterly destroyed all the people with the edge of the sword. **9** But Saul and the people spared Agag, and the best of the sheep, and of the oxen, and of the fatlings, and the lambs, and all that was good, and would not utterly destroy them: but every thing that was vile and refuse, that they destroyed utterly. **10** Then came the word of the Lord unto Samuel, saying, **11** It repenteth me that I have set up Saul to be king: for he is turned back from following me, and hath not performed my commandments. And it grieved Samuel; and he cried unto the Lord all night. **12** And when Samuel rose early to meet Saul in the morning, it was told Samuel, saying, Saul came to Carmel, and, behold, he set him up a place, and is gone about, and passed on, and gone down to Gilgal. **13** And Samuel came to Saul: and Saul said unto him, Blessed be thou of the Lord: I have performed the commandment of the Lord. **14** And Samuel said, What meaneth then this bleating of the sheep in mine ears, and the lowing of the oxen which I hear? **15** And Saul said, They have brought them from the Amalekites: for the people spared the best of the sheep and of the oxen, to sacrifice unto the Lord thy God; and the rest we have utterly destroyed. **16** Then Samuel said unto Saul, Stay, and I will tell thee what the Lord hath said to me this night. And he said unto him, Say on. **17** And Samuel said, When thou wast little in thine own sight, wast thou not made the head of the tribes of Israel, and the Lord anointed thee king over Israel? **18** And the Lord sent thee on a journey, and said, Go and utterly destroy the sinners the Amalekites, and fight against them until they be consumed. **19** Wherefore then didst thou not obey the voice of the Lord, but didst fly upon the spoil, and didst evil in the sight of the Lord? **20** And Saul said unto Samuel, Yea, I have obeyed the voice of the Lord, and have gone the way which the Lord sent me, and have brought Agag the king of Amalek, and have utterly destroyed the Amalekites. **21** But the people took of the spoil, sheep and oxen, the chief of the things which should have been utterly destroyed, to sacrifice unto the Lord thy God in Gilgal. **22** And Samuel said, Hath the Lord as great delight in burnt offerings and sacrifices, as in obeying the voice of the Lord? Behold, to obey is better than sacrifice, and to hearken than the fat of rams. **23** For rebellion is as the sin of witchcraft, and stubbornness is as iniquity and idolatry. Because thou hast rejected the word of the Lord, he hath also rejected thee from being king.

24 And Saul said unto Samuel, I have sinned: for I have transgressed the commandment of the Lord, and thy words: because I feared the people, and obeyed their voice. **25** Now therefore, I pray thee, pardon my sin, and turn again with me, that I may worship the Lord. **26** And Samuel said unto Saul, I will not return with thee: for thou hast rejected the word of the Lord, and the Lord hath rejected thee from being king over Israel. **27** And as Samuel turned about to go

away, he laid hold upon the skirt of his mantle, and it rent.
28 And Samuel said unto him, The Lord hath rent the
kingdom of Israel from thee this day, and hath given it to a
neighbour of thine, that is better than thou. 29 And also the
Strength of Israel will not lie nor repent: for he is not a man,
that he should repent. 30 Then he said, I have sinned: yet
honour me now, I pray thee, before the elders of my people,
and before Israel, and turn again with me, that I may
worship the Lord thy God. 31 So Samuel turned again after
Saul; and Saul worshipped the Lord. 32 Then said Samuel,
Bring ye hither to me Agag the king of the Amalekites. And
Agag came unto him delicately. And Agag said, Surely the
bitterness of death is past. 33 And Samuel said, As thy sword
hath made women childless, so shall thy mother be childless
among women. And Samuel hewed Agag in pieces before the
Lord in Gilgal. 34 Then Samuel went to Ramah; and Saul
went up to his house to Gibeah of Saul. 35 And Samuel came
no more to see Saul until the day of his death: nevertheless
Samuel mourned for Saul: and the Lord repented that he had
made Saul king over Israel.

Now, let us look at the case of Saul, king of Israel. In 1st Samuel chapters 8, 10 and 15, we see that Saul was a product of agitation by the children of Israel. The children of Israel desired to be like other kingdoms and other nations, to have a human king over them. Samuel was grieved that they desired a human king and complained to God about it. God told him not to worry himself as he was not the person they were after, even though they mentioned Samuel's sons as an excuse, stating that Samuel's sons were not like their father. But God told him that the real point was that they were rejecting Him as their King and so, needed a human king. In the search for a king for Israel, Saul was chosen.

SAUL, FIRST KING OF ISRAEL

At this point in time, Saul was a very timid and shy person, though tall in stature and with all it took to be a physically strong leader. He was humble, timid yet God had chosen him to be the king of Israel. But as he became king, his whole system changed.

Of course, a change in political and financial position changes people, for those who allow themselves to be changed. One can either change for the better or for the worse. In Saul's case, he was changed for the worse. He became full of himself, and even became impatient with the prophet that had anointed him king.

When it was time to sacrifice, Saul waited for the prophet to come and perform the sacrifice but when the prophet didn't come on time, he went ahead and performed the sacrifice himself; a duty that was not in his purview to do. He was not a priest, he was not even a Levite, he wasn't from the priestly order yet he went and offered a sacrifice. That was his first offence.

His second offence happened when God gave him an assignment to destroy all the Amalekites as punishment for what they did to Israel during the Exodus. "Destroy all!" was the commandment from God. But instead of obeying, he saved their king, Agag, destroyed all the feeble and useless animals and things and saved the best portions as spoil for himself and his soldiers. This was contrary to what God had asked him to do.

When Samuel the prophet questioned him about his disobedience to God's directive, he rationalized his action by saying that he had brought back the good portion for sacrifice to God. Samuel then told him that to obey is better than sacrifice. He should have simply obeyed what God had asked him to do by obliterating everything that is Amalekites-related and wiping out the Amalekites from the face of the earth. If he had done this, he would have been in God's good books forever.

That was the beginning of the end of his reign. That event signalled the demise of his kingdom and as a result of his actions, God took His hand off him. That particular incident also infuriated Samuel because he had seen in Saul, a humble man who would carry out everything that God had asked him to do but alas, he failed woefully. Samuel was greatly pained and the Bible said that after that encounter, Samuel never set his eyes on Saul again until he, Samuel, died.

Goliath And The Failure Of Saul

1 Samuel 17 (KJV)

David Kills Goliath

> *1 Now the Philistines gathered together their armies to battle, and were gathered together at Shochoh, which belongeth to Judah, and pitched between Shochoh and Azekah, in Ephesdammim. 2 And Saul and the men of Israel were gathered together, and pitched by the valley of Elah, and set the battle in array against the Philistines. 3 And the*

SAUL, FIRST KING OF ISRAEL

Philistines stood on a mountain on the one side, and Israel stood on a mountain on the other side: and there was a valley between them. **4** And there went out a champion out of the camp of the Philistines, named Goliath, of Gath, whose height was six cubits and a span. **5** And he had an helmet of brass upon his head, and he was armed with a coat of mail; and the weight of the coat was five thousand shekels of brass. **6** And he had greaves of brass upon his legs, and a target of brass between his shoulders. **7** And the staff of his spear was like a weaver's beam; and his spear's head weighed six hundred shekels of iron: and one bearing a shield went before him. **8** And he stood and cried unto the armies of Israel, and said unto them, Why are ye come out to set your battle in array? Am not I a Philistine, and ye servants to Saul? choose you a man for you, and let him come down to me. **9** If he be able to fight with me, and to kill me, then will we be your servants: but if I prevail against him, and kill him, then shall ye be our servants, and serve us. **10** And the Philistine said, I defy the armies of Israel this day; give me a man, that we may fight together. **11** When Saul and all Israel heard those words of the Philistine, they were dismayed, and greatly afraid.

12 Now David was the son of that Ephrathite of Bethlehemjudah, whose name was Jesse; and he had eight sons: and the man went among men for an old man in the days of Saul. **13** And the three eldest sons of Jesse went and followed Saul to the battle: and the names of his three sons that went to the battle were Eliab the firstborn, and next unto him Abinadab, and the third Shammah. **14** And David was the youngest: and the three eldest followed Saul. **15** But David went and returned from Saul to feed his father's sheep at Bethlehem. **16** And the Philistine drew near morning and evening, and presented himself forty days. **17** And Jesse said unto David his son, Take now for thy brethren an ephah of this parched corn, and these ten loaves, and run to the camp to thy brethren; **18** And carry these ten cheeses unto the captain of their thousand, and look how thy brethren fare, and take their pledge. **19** Now Saul, and they, and all the men of Israel, were in the valley of Elah, fighting with the Philistines. **20** And David rose up early in the morning, and left the sheep with a keeper, and took, and went, as Jesse had commanded him; and he came to the trench, as the host was going forth to the fight, and shouted for the battle. **21** For Israel and the Philistines had put the battle in array, army against army. **22** And David left his carriage in the hand of the keeper of the carriage, and ran into the army, and came and saluted his brethren. **23** And as he talked with them, behold, there came up the champion, the Philistine of Gath, Goliath by name, out of the armies of the Philistines, and spake according to the same words: and David heard them. **24** And all the men of Israel, when they saw the man, fled from him, and were sore afraid. **25** And the men of Israel said, Have ye seen this man that is come up? surely to defy Israel is he come up: and it shall be, that the man who killeth him, the king will enrich him with great riches, and will give him his daughter, and make his father's house free in Israel. **26** And David spake to the men that stood by him, saying, What shall be done to the man that killeth this Philistine, and taketh away the reproach from Israel? for who is this uncircumcised Philistine, that he should defy the armies of the living God? **27** And the people answered him after this manner, saying, So shall it be done to the man that killeth him. **28** And Eliab his eldest brother heard when he spake unto the men; and Eliab's anger was kindled against David, and he said, Why camest thou down hither? and with whom hast thou left those few sheep in the wilderness? I know thy pride, and the naughtiness of thine heart; for thou art come down that thou mightest see the battle. **29** And David said, What have I now done? Is there not a cause? **30** And he turned from him toward another, and spake after the same manner: and the people answered him again after the former manner.

31 And when the words were heard which David spake, they rehearsed them before Saul: and he sent for him. **32** And David said to Saul, Let no man's heart fail because of him; thy servant will go and fight with this Philistine. **33** And Saul said to David, Thou art not able to go against this Philistine to fight with him: for thou art but a youth, and he a man of war from his youth. **34** And David said unto Saul, Thy servant kept his father's sheep, and there came a lion, and a bear, and took a lamb out of the flock: **35** And I went out after him, and smote him, and delivered it out of his mouth: and when he arose against me, I caught him by his beard, and smote him, and slew him. **36** Thy servant slew both the lion and the bear: and this uncircumcised Philistine shall be as one of them, seeing he hath defied the armies of the living God. **37** David said moreover, The Lord that delivered me out of the paw of the lion, and out of the paw of the bear, he will deliver me out of the hand of this Philistine. And Saul said unto David, Go, and the Lord be with thee. **38** And Saul armed David with his armour, and he put an helmet of brass upon his head; also he armed him with a coat of mail. **39** And David girded his sword upon his armour, and he assayed to go; for he had not proved it. And David said unto Saul, I cannot go with these; for I have not proved them. And David put them off him. **40** And he took his staff in his hand, and chose him five smooth stones out of the brook, and put them in a shepherd's bag which he had, even in a scrip; and his sling was in his hand: and he drew near to the Philistine. **41** And the Philistine came on and drew near unto David; and the man that bare the shield went before him. **42** And when the Philistine looked about, and saw David, he disdained him: for he was but a youth, and ruddy, and of a fair countenance. **43** And the Philistine said unto David, Am I a dog, that thou comest to me with staves? And the Philistine cursed David by his gods. **44** And the Philistine said to David, Come to me, and I will give thy flesh unto the fowls of the air, and to the beasts of the field. **45** Then said David to the Philistine, Thou comest to me with a sword, and with a spear, and with a shield: but I come to thee in the name of the Lord of hosts, the God of the armies of Israel, whom thou hast defied. **46** This day will the Lord deliver thee into mine hand; and I will smite thee, and take thine head from thee; and I will give the carcases of the host of the Philistines this day unto the fowls of the air, and to the wild beasts of the earth; that all the earth may know that there is a God in Israel. **47** And all this assembly shall know that the Lord saveth not with sword and spear: for the battle is the Lord's, and he will give you into our hands. **48** And it came to pass, when the Philistine arose, and came and drew nigh to meet David, that David hasted, and ran toward the army to meet the Philistine. **49** And David put his hand in his bag, and took thence a stone, and slang it, and smote the Philistine in his forehead, that the stone sunk into his forehead; and he fell upon his face to the earth. **50** So David prevailed over the Philistine with a sling and with a stone, and smote the Philistine, and slew him; but there was no sword in the hand of David. **51** Therefore David ran, and stood upon the Philistine, and took his sword, and drew it out of the sheath thereof, and slew him, and cut off his head therewith. And when the Philistines saw their champion was dead, they fled. **52** And the men of Israel and of Judah arose, and shouted, and pursued the Philistines, until thou come to the valley, and to the gates of Ekron. And the wounded of the Philistines fell down by the way to Shaaraim, even unto Gath, and unto Ekron. **53** And the children of Israel returned from chasing after the Philistines, and they spoiled their tents. **54** And David took the head of the Philistine, and brought it to Jerusalem; but he put his armour in his tent. **55** And when Saul saw David go forth against the Philistine, he said unto Abner, the captain of the host, Abner, whose son is this youth? And Abner said, As thy soul liveth, O king, I cannot tell. **56** And the king said, Enquire thou whose son the stripling is. **57** And as David returned from the slaughter of the Philistine, Abner took him, and brought him before Saul with the head of the Philistine in his hand. **58** And Saul said to him, Whose son art thou, thou young man? And David answered, I am the son of thy servant Jesse the Bethlehemite.

1 Samuel 18 (KJV)

Jonathan's Covenant with David

18 And it came to pass, when he had made an end of speaking unto Saul, that the soul of Jonathan was knit with the soul of David, and Jonathan loved him as his own soul. **2** And Saul took him that day, and would let him go no more home to his father's house. **3** Then Jonathan and David made a covenant, because he loved him as his own soul. **4** And Jonathan stripped himself of the robe that was upon him, and gave it to David, and his garments, even to his sword, and to his bow, and to his girdle. **5** And David went out whithersoever Saul sent him, and behaved himself wisely: and Saul set him over the men of war, and he was accepted in the sight of all the people, and also in the sight of Saul's servants.

Saul Becomes Jealous of David

6 And it came to pass as they came, when David was returned from the slaughter of the Philistine, that the women came out of all cities of Israel, singing and dancing, to meet king Saul, with tabrets, with joy, and with instruments of musick. **7** And the women answered one another as they played, and said, Saul hath slain his thousands, and David his ten thousands. **8** And Saul was very wroth, and the saying displeased him; and he said, They have ascribed unto David ten thousands, and to me they have ascribed but thousands: and what can he have more *but the kingdom? 9 And Saul eyed David from that day and forward. 10 And it came to pass on the morrow, that the evil spirit from God came upon Saul, and he prophesied in the midst of the house: and David played with his hand, as at other times: and there was a javelin in Saul's hand. 11 And Saul cast the javelin; for he said, I will smite David even to the wall with it. And David avoided out of his presence twice. 12 And Saul was afraid of David, because the Lord was with him, and was departed from Saul*

Saul's problem was really with God then the incident of Goliath happened.

This was a man that taunted Israel to the point where Saul, his mighty men and his commanders went into hiding; they could not stand before Goliath. Goliath had a field day, taunting and making mockery of Israel and thereby, making mockery of the God of Israel.

It was at this point that this young lad, David, a shepherd boy, untrained in warfare and unskilled in handling military weapons, came along and dislodged Goliath with the weapons he knew best. By calling on the Name of the Lord and using a stone and a sling, he crushed Goliath.

After Goliath died, he used the giant's sword to cut off his head. As he lifted Goliath's head, all the fearful soldiers of Israel awoke to their responsibility. They pursued their enemies and the Philistines were routed and thoroughly defeated because David had slaughtered their strongman.

SAUL, FIRST KING OF ISRAEL

Saul should have been very happy with David, and maybe he was, for removing shame and reproach from Israel, but he became enraged when he heard the lyrics which the women sang. As the soldiers were returning from the slaughter of the Philistines and having heard the news of the bravery of David, the women burst forth into singing that Saul had killed his thousands and David his ten thousands. They promoted David far above Saul and this rattled him.

It was the women who composed and created the songs which they sang and David had no hand whatsoever in it. He did not compose the lyrics neither did they have his approval to sing it. It was a spontaneous eruption of song which spread all over Jerusalem.

Saul was enraged. Enraged at the elevation of David above him. Instead of dragging issues with the women who had composed and sang the song, he chose to be vexed with the young man, David, who had just done Israel a wonderful service. He swore to destroy him.
He became so embittered against David that the unforgiving spirit overwhelmed him so strongly that all he could do was think of how to destroy David.

Now, look at this sequence of events. In all the problems that Saul had, David had never played a part. His problems started between him and God and all he should have done was to sort it out with God in a proper way, but he didn't. Then the same David that did God, Israel and Saul a great favour by removing the shame and reproach

73

of Goliath from the people of Israel was rewarded with hatred and hunted like a criminal. Why?

David had become the recipient of such hatred, bitterness and resentment because of mere songs of praise.
In subsequent years and on several occasions, when David had the opportunity to kill Saul, he did not; rather, he made Saul to see that he could have killed him but didn't. Whenever such happened, Saul would behave as if he had repented of his wickedness, only to turn around the next minute and chase after David. He had become beclouded by this wicked spirit of resentment.

The Slaughter Of The Priests Of God

1 Samuel 21 (KJV)

David Flees from Saul

> 1 Then came David to Nob to Ahimelech the priest: and Ahimelech was afraid at the meeting of David, and said unto him, Why art thou alone, and no man with thee? 2 And David said unto Ahimelech the priest, The king hath commanded me a business, and hath said unto me, Let no man know any thing of the business whereabout I send thee, and what I have commanded thee: and I have appointed my servants to such and such a place. 3 Now therefore what is under thine hand? give me five loaves of bread in mine hand, or what there is present. 4 And the priest answered David, and said, There is no common bread under mine hand, but there is hallowed bread; if the young men have kept themselves at least from women. 5 And David answered the priest, and said unto him, Of a truth women have been kept from us

about these three days, since I came out, and the vessels of the young men are holy, and the bread is in a manner common, yea, though it were sanctified this day in the vessel. 6 So the priest gave him hallowed bread: for there was no bread there but the shewbread, that was taken from before the Lord, to put hot bread in the day when it was taken away. 7 Now a certain man of the servants of Saul was there that day, detained before the Lord; and his name was Doeg, an Edomite, the chiefest of the herdmen that belonged to Saul. 8 And David said unto Ahimelech, And is there not here under thine hand spear or sword? for I have neither brought my sword nor my weapons with me, because the king's business required haste. 9 And the priest said, The sword of Goliath the Philistine, whom thou slewest in the valley of Elah, behold, it is here wrapped in a cloth behind the ephod: if thou wilt take that, take it: for there is no other save that here. And David said, There is none like that; give it me. 10 And David arose, and fled that day for fear of Saul, and went to Achish the king of Gath.?

1 Samuel 22 Verses 6 to 23

Saul Kills the Priests of Nob

6 When Saul heard that David was discovered, and the men that were with him, (now Saul abode in Gibeah under a tree in Ramah, having his spear in his hand, and all his servants were standing about him;) 7 Then Saul said unto his servants that stood about him, Hear now, ye Benjamites; will the son of Jesse give every one of you fields and vineyards, and make you all captains of thousands, and captains of hundreds; 8 That all of you have conspired against me, and there is none that sheweth me that my son hath made a league with the son of Jesse, and there is none of you that is sorry for me, or sheweth

unto me that my son hath stirred up my servant against me, to lie in wait, as at this day? **9** Then answered Doeg the Edomite, which was set over the servants of Saul, and said, I saw the son of Jesse coming to Nob, to Ahimelech the son of Ahitub. **10** And he enquired of the Lord for him, and gave him victuals, and gave him the sword of Goliath the Philistine. **11** Then the king sent to call Ahimelech the priest, the son of Ahitub, and all his father's house, the priests that were in Nob: and they came all of them to the king. **12** And Saul said, Hear now, thou son of Ahitub. And he answered, Here I am, my lord. **13** And Saul said unto him, Why have ye conspired against me, thou and the son of Jesse, in that thou hast given him bread, and a sword, and hast enquired of God for him, that he should rise against me, to lie in wait, as at this day? **14** Then Ahimelech answered the king, and said, And who is so faithful among all thy servants as David, which is the king's son in law, and goeth at thy bidding, and is honourable in thine house? **15** Did I then begin to enquire of God for him? be it far from me: let not the king impute anything unto his servant, nor to all the house of my father: for thy servant knew nothing of all this, less or more. **16** And the king said, Thou shalt surely die, Ahimelech, thou, and all thy father's house. **17** And the king said unto the footmen that stood about him, Turn, and slay the priests of the Lord; because their hand also is with David, and because they knew when he fled, and did not shew it to me. But the servants of the king would not put forth their hand to fall upon the priests of the Lord. **18** And the king said to Doeg, Turn thou, and fall upon the priests. And Doeg the Edomite turned, and he fell upon the priests, and slew on that day fourscore and five persons that did wear a linen ephod. **19** And Nob, the city of the priests, smote he with the edge of the sword, both men and women, children and sucklings, and oxen, and asses, and sheep, with the edge of the sword. **20** And one of the sons of Ahimelech the son of Ahitub, named

Abiathar, escaped, and fled after David. **21** And Abiathar shewed David that Saul had slain the Lord's priests. **22** And David said unto Abiathar, I knew it that day, when Doeg the Edomite was there, that he would surely tell Saul: I have occasioned the death of all the persons of thy father's house. **23** Abide thou with me, fear not: for he that seeketh my life seeketh thy life: but with me thou shalt be in safeguard.

It so happened that as David ran to some priests in the course of hiding from Saul, David and his men had to be fed with priestly portions because they were starving. Saul, on hearing this, approached the priests and when they refused to disclose David's movement to Saul, he ordered the slaughtering of the priests; eighty-five of them were killed.

Because of this wicked spirit of bitterness that had possessed Saul, committing an abomination by killing ordained and anointed priests of God meant nothing to him. Although the Israeli soldiers with him frowned and dissociated themselves from such abomination, Saul forged ahead and used Doeg, a foreigner, to commit such a dastardly act.

These happened because of his bitterness and vengefulness towards David- whose only sin against Saul was that he stood with God to remove a great reproach from Israel and afterwards, had the misfortune of being praised by the women of Jerusalem higher and above Saul.

He continued pursuing David who ran from one cave to another and from one nation to another. He even ran to the enemies of Israel for protection with all his men, family members, friends and loyalists.

1 Samuel 22 (KJV)

> 1 David therefore departed thence, and escaped to the cave Adullam: and when his brethren and all his father's house heard it, they went down thither to him. [2] And every one that was in distress, and every one that was in debt, and every one that was discontented, gathered themselves unto him; and he became a captain over them: and there were with him about four hundred men. [3] And David went thence to Mizpeh of Moab: and he said unto the king of Moab, Let my father and my mother, I pray thee, come forth, and be with you, till I know what God will do for me.

The Bible says that men who were in distress, debtors and the discontented gathered around him and became his followers, running from one place to the other like fugitives. But Saul, instead of going to God for forgiveness and repenting of his failure to do the biddings of God, left the business of governing Israel and was running around also, chasing David to kill him. This is what the unforgiving spirit can do to a man.

Such a man, under its influence, can be so overwhelmed by this spirit and become jealous over a man for nothing. Just because the man became successful, they would become jealous and begin saying, "Why should it be him? Why should he be in the position that he is in? He must be cut down from that position."

Many of us are in that situation, embittered over nothing. The man has done nothing to you; he did not stop you from climbing your own ladder, he did not! He did not influence your situation neither did he participate in keeping you where you are today but then you're angry, angry with him for being successful. You are so angry you have decided you must deal with him, you must destroy him, you must pull him down, but for what?

There are so many people that are like Saul, who have issues to sort out with God but who instead of going to God in humility and in repentance, pleading with God to have mercy on them and to deliver them from the situation in which they are in, are rather pursuing shadows, haunting people who have done nothing to them.

The Need To Forgive Ourselves

I have come to the understanding that for us to be able to come to the point wherein we can be cleansed of this terrible unforgiving spirit, we have to first forgive ourselves. You have to forgive yourself first in order to have the capacity to forgive others.

Saul never forgave himself; he felt he was now a failure who could not fight Goliath. Unknown to them, the women rubbed it in further by singing that he had only killed thousands while David had killed tens of thousands and that was the final blow for his degeneration. He therefore chose to avenge his injured pride instead of repenting and forgiving himself and coming before God in humility. He could not forgive himself and therefore could not forgive any other. Even though David did nothing to him, he kept pursuing David until he himself was consumed.

The Death Of Saul

1 Samuel 31 (KJV)

1 Now the Philistines fought against Israel: and the men of Israel fled from before the Philistines, and fell down slain in mount Gilboa. [2] And the Philistines followed hard upon Saul and upon his sons; and the Philistines slew Jonathan, and Abinadab, and Melchishua, Saul's sons. [3] And the battle went sore against Saul, and the archers hit him; and he was sore wounded of the archers. [4] Then said Saul unto his armour bearer, Draw thy sword, and thrust me through therewith; lest these uncircumcised come and thrust me through, and abuse me. But his armour bearer would not; for he was sore afraid. Therefore Saul took a sword, and fell upon it. [5] And when his armour bearer saw that Saul was dead, he fell likewise upon his sword, and died with him. [6] So Saul died, and his three sons, and his armour bearer, and all his men, that same day together. [7] And when the men of Israel that were on the other side of the valley, and they that were on the other side Jordan, saw that the men of Israel fled, and that Saul and his sons were dead, they forsook the cities, and fled; and the Philistines came and dwelt in them. [8] And it came to pass on the morrow, when the Philistines came to strip the slain, that they found Saul and his three sons fallen in mount Gilboa. [9] And they cut off his head, and stripped off his armour, and sent into the land of the Philistines round about, to publish it in the house of their idols, and among

the people. ¹⁰ And they put his armour in the house of Ashtaroth: and they fastened his body to the wall of Bethshan. ¹¹ And when the inhabitants of Jabeshgilead heard of that which the Philistines had done to Saul; ¹² All the valiant men arose, and went all night, and took the body of Saul and the bodies of his sons from the wall of Bethshan, and came to Jabesh, and burnt them there. ¹³ And they took their bones, and buried them under a tree at Jabesh, and fasted seven days.

At the end, Saul suffered such a terrible defeat at the hands of Israel's enemies that he had to beg his armour bearer to help him die. When his armour bearer refused, he fell upon his sword and committed suicide. What a terrible death!

We need to know that unforgiveness breeds nothing but death and destruction. Sit down and ask yourself, "This man I am pursuing or this woman whom I have vowed to destroy, what has he/she really done to me." Then check yourself and recall all the evil that you have done to people and much more to God, yet God has forgiven you. Why are you now finding it difficult to forgive yourself?

You need to forgive yourself so that you will have the capacity to also forgive others. You need to forgive those whom you think offended you; it is in your interest so that your Father in heaven will also forgive your trespasses against Him. See what our Lord Jesus said in **Matthew Chapter 6 verses 12 to 15**:

¹² And forgive us our debts, as we forgive our debtors. ¹³ And lead us not into temptation, but deliver us from evil: For

thine is the kingdom, and the power, and the glory, forever. Amen. [14] *For if ye forgive men their trespasses, your heavenly Father will also forgive you:* [15] *But if ye forgive not men their trespasses, neither will your Father forgive your trespasses.*

The point is that you are doing yourself a great favour by forgiving others- yes yourself, not others. Unforgiveness is a cankerworm that eats into a person, destroys the fabrics of their being, and leaves them with high blood pressure and other terrible health conditions. These health issues arise because there is inner turmoil, loss of happiness, loss of joy; just inner struggles. The individual becomes consumed by thoughts of revenge and full of the gall of bitterness and the end thereof is nothing but death.

Check out all that have this unforgiving spirit and all those focused on exacting revenge, (in some cases, for nothing done against them); they end up being consumed by the gall of bitterness that has welled up inside of them.

May the good Lord deliver us from unforgiving spirit. May He save us from every gall of bitterness. And may He save us and grant us the ability to forgive ourselves and the capacity to forgive others. Amen.

CHAPTER 7

JOAB, THE COMMANDER OF DAVID'S ARMY

Embittered by His Failures to Do the Right Thing

Joab was a great warrior who had been with David from the days of his fugitive living— when he was living from one cave to the other. He had been with him when David was running away from Saul, king of Israel. At that time, David's life had been in danger and a few men had rallied round him and formed a team with David as their leader. Throughout the period when David was a fugitive running away from the antics of Saul, this team went everywhere with him (1 Samuel 22: 1 and 2).

1 Samuel 22 (KJV)

1 David therefore departed thence, and escaped to the cave Adullam: and when his brethren and all his father's house heard it, they went down thither to him. 2 And every one that was in distress, and every one that was in debt, and every one that was discontented, gathered themselves unto him; and he became a captain over them: and there were with him about four hundred men.

Joab and his two brothers, Abishai and Asahel, were a vital part of this team and Joab rose to become a commander of David's army. Joab was also the son of Zeruiah, David's sister thus he was David's nephew. He was very close to David and constantly put his life on the line for his safety. Whenever David had rough times, Joab was always there to defend the integrity of David and his life. On certain occasions, he went against the will and wishes of David in order to destroy any seeming danger that was to come to David. The case of Absalom's rebellion is a very good example.

2 Samuel 18:1 -17, 31-33 (KJV)

[1] And David numbered the people that were with him, and set captains of thousands, and captains of hundreds over them. [2] And David sent forth a third part of the people under the hand of Joab and a third part under the hand of Abishai the son of Zeruiah, Joab's brother, and a third part under the hand of Ittai the Gittite. And the king said unto the people, I will surely go forth with you myself also. [3] But the people answered, Thou shalt not go forth: for if we flee away, they will not care for us; neither if half of us die, will they care for us: but now thou art worth ten thousand of us: therefore now it is better that thou succour us out of the city. [4] And the king said unto them, What seemeth you best I will do. And the king stood by the gate side, and all the people came out by hundreds and by thousands. [5] And the king commanded Joab and Abishai and Ittai, saying, Deal gently for my sake with the young man, even with Absalom. And all the people heard when the king gave all the captains charge concerning Absalom. [6] So the people went out into the field against Israel: and the battle was in the wood of Ephraim; [7] Where the people of Israel were slain before the servants of David, and there was there a great slaughter that day of twenty thousand men. [8] For the battle was there scattered over the face of all the country: and the wood devoured more people that day than the sword devoured. [9] And Absalom met the servants of David. And Absalom rode upon a mule, and the mule went under the thick boughs of a great oak, and his head caught hold of the oak, and he was taken

up between the heaven and the earth; and the mule that was under him went away. [10] And a certain man saw it, and told Joab, and said, Behold, I saw Absalom hanged in an oak. [11] And Joab said unto the man that told him, And, behold, thou sawest him, and why didst thou not smite him there to the ground? and I would have given thee ten shekels of silver, and a girdle. [12] And the man said unto Joab, Though I should receive a thousand shekels of silver in mine hand, yet would I not put forth mine hand against the king's son: for in our hearing the king charged thee and Abishai and Ittai, saying, Beware that none touch the young man Absalom. [13] Otherwise I should have wrought falsehood against mine own life: for there is no matter hid from the king, and thou thyself wouldest have set thyself against me. [14] Then said Joab, I may not tarry thus with thee. And he took three darts in his hand, and thrust them through the heart of Absalom, while he was yet alive in the midst of the oak. [15] And ten young men that bare Joab's armour compassed about and smote Absalom, and slew him. [16] And Joab blew the trumpet, and the people returned from pursuing after Israel: for Joab held back the people. [17] And they took Absalom, and cast him into a great pit in the wood, and laid a very great heap of stones upon him: and all Israel fled everyone to his tent.

[31] And, behold, Cushi came; and Cushi said, Tidings, my lord the king: for the LORD hath avenged thee this day of all them that rose up against thee. [32] And the king said unto Cushi, Is the young man Absalom safe? And Cushi answered, The enemies of my lord the king, and all that rise against thee to do thee hurt, be as that young man is. [33] And the king was much moved, and went up to the chamber over the gate, and wept: and as he went, thus he said, O my son Absalom, my son, my son Absalom! would God I had died for thee, O Absalom, my son, my son!

Source Of Joab's Bitterness

Now, Joab had a problem. His problem developed because he became very antagonistic and unforgiving towards Abner. Abner was the commander of King Saul's army. Abner and Joab had a lot of fights during the time when King Saul was in pursuit of David and even after the death of Saul when Abner fought to enthrone one of the sons of Saul, Ish-bosheth, as king of Israel.

On a certain occasion, Abner and the soldiers under his command had an encounter with the army of David led by Joab and Joab's younger brother, Asahel, went in pursuit of Abner. Of course, Abner was a powerful and well-trained soldier. For him to have been the commander of Saul's army, it meant he was above average and was actually one of the best, if not the best.

Asahel, as typical of the sons of Zeruiah, was also a great man of war. In the chronology of the great warriors of David as recorded in 2 Samuel 23 verse 24, Asahel was numbered amongst the thirty mighty men of David.

Asahel pursued after Abner and Abner called out to him, imploring him to go back:

2 Samuel 2: 8 -32 (KJV)

David Fights against the Forces of Saul
8 But Abner the son of Ner, captain of Saul's host, took Ishbosheth the son of Saul, and brought him over to

86

Mahanaim; **9** And made him king over Gilead, and over the Ashurites, and over Jezreel, and over Ephraim, and over Benjamin, and over all Israel. **10** Ishbosheth Saul's son was forty years old when he began to reign over Israel, and reigned two years. But the house of Judah followed David. **11** And the time that David was king in Hebron over the house of Judah was seven years and six months. **12** And Abner the son of Ner, and the servants of Ishbosheth the son of Saul, went out from Mahanaim to Gibeon. **13** And Joab the son of Zeruiah, and the servants of David, went out, and met together by the pool of Gibeon: and they sat down, the one on the one side of the pool, and the other on the other side of the pool. **14** And Abner said to Joab, Let the young men now arise, and play before us. And Joab said, Let them arise. **15** Then there arose and went over by number twelve of Benjamin, which pertained to Ishbosheth the son of Saul, and twelve of the servants of David. **16** And they caught everyone his fellow by the head, and thrust his sword in his fellow's side; so they fell down together: wherefore that place was called Helkathhazzurim, which is in Gibeon. **17** And there was a very sore battle that day; and Abner was beaten, and the men of Israel, before the servants of David.

18 And there were three sons of Zeruiah there, Joab, and Abishai, and Asahel: and Asahel was as light of foot as a wild roe. **19** And Asahel pursued after Abner; and in going he turned not to the right hand nor to the left from following Abner. **20** Then Abner looked behind him, and said, Art thou Asahel? And he answered, I am. **21** And Abner said to him, Turn thee aside to thy right hand or to thy left, and lay thee hold on one of the young men, and take thee his armour. But Asahel would not turn aside from following of him. **22** And Abner said again to Asahel, Turn thee aside from following me: wherefore should I smite thee to the ground? how then should I hold up my face to Joab thy brother? **23** Howbeit he refused to turn aside: wherefore Abner with the hinder end of the spear smote him under the fifth rib, that the spear *came out behind him; and he fell down there, and died in the same place: and it came to pass, that as many as came to the place where Asahel fell down and died stood still. 24 Joab also and Abishai pursued after Abner: and the sun went down when they were come to the hill of Ammah, that lieth before Giah by the way of the wilderness of Gibeon. 25 And the children of Benjamin gathered themselves together after Abner, and became one troop, and stood on the top of an hill. 26 Then Abner called to Joab, and said, Shall the sword devour for ever? knowest thou not that it will be bitterness in the latter end? how long shall it be then, ere thou bid the people return from following their brethren? 27 And Joab said, As God liveth, unless thou hadst spoken, surely then in the morning the people had gone up every one from following his brother. 28 So Joab blew a trumpet, and all the people stood still, and pursued after Israel no more, neither fought they any more. 29 And Abner and his men walked all that night through the plain, and passed over Jordan, and went through all Bithron, and they came to Mahanaim. 30 And Joab returned from following Abner: and when he had gathered all the people together, there lacked of David's servants nineteen men and Asahel. 31 But the servants of David had smitten of Benjamin, and of Abner's men, so that three hundred and threescore men died. 32 And they took up Asahel, and buried him in the sepulchre of his father, which was in Bethlehem. And Joab and his men went all night, and they came to Hebron at break of day.*

Abner called out to Asahel to go back. He was basically saying, I do not know how I would face your brother if I dealt with you; go back and stop pursuing me. But Asahel would not stop.

Joab, knowing the military pedigree of Abner, should have called his brother back from pursuing Abner, but he did not. The result of this was that Abner struck Asahel dead. Instead of dealing with his negligence and inaction, Joab became bitter and, together with his other brother Abishai, pursued Abner to avenge the death of their brother, Asahel. When he failed to exact the revenge immediately, he bided time and waited for an opportunity to avenge the death of his brother.

If he had forgiven himself for not calling back his brother from the pursuit of Abner, maybe he would have had the capacity to forgive Abner as well. But he had not. He did not forgive himself and so he lay in wait, seeking for an opportunity to avenge the death of his brother.

2 Samuel Chapters 2 and 3 are very instructive about what led to the death of Asahel and how Joab became greatly offended by the death of his brother. This offence brought out a new dimension of resentment in him.

One can't say whether he was blaming himself for allowing his brother to pursue such a great warrior as Abner or whether he was blaming himself for his own negligence and thereby, finding it difficult to come to terms with it. He just could not come to terms with forgiving himself. It is imperative that for you to forgive others you have to have the capacity to first forgive yourself. And so he planned and waited for the opportunity to come for him to get back at Abner, not just to injure Abner, but to kill him. He waited for such opportunity to come and did not waste it once it came.

Joab Satisfies The Spirit Of Unforgiveness

2 Samuel 3: 6 – 39 (KJV)

Abner Plans a League with David

> **6** And it came to pass, while there was war between the house of Saul and the house of David, that Abner made himself strong for the house of Saul. **7** And Saul had a concubine, whose name was Rizpah, the daughter of Aiah: and Ishbosheth said to Abner, Wherefore hast thou gone in unto my father's concubine? **8** Then was Abner very wroth for the words of Ishbosheth, and said, Am I a dog's head, which against Judah do shew kindness this day unto the house of Saul thy father, to his brethren, and to his friends, and have not delivered thee into the hand of David, that thou chargest me to day with a fault concerning this woman? **9** So do God to Abner, and more also, except, as the Lord hath sworn to David, even so I do to him; **10** To translate the kingdom from the house of Saul, and to set up the throne of David over Israel and over Judah, from Dan even to Beersheba. **11** And he could not answer Abner a word again, because he feared him. **12** And Abner sent messengers to David on his behalf, saying, Whose is the land? saying also, Make thy league with me, and, behold, my hand shall be with thee, to bring about all Israel unto thee. **13** And he said, Well; I will make a league with thee: but one thing I require of thee, that is, Thou shalt not see my face, except thou first bring Michal Saul's daughter, when thou comest to see my face. **14** And David sent messengers to Ishbosheth Saul's son, saying, Deliver me my wife Michal, which I espoused to me for an hundred foreskins of the Philistines. **15** And Ishbosheth sent, and took her from her husband, even from Phaltiel the son of Laish. **16** And her husband went with her along weeping behind her to Bahurim. Then

JOAB, THE COMMANDER OF DAVID'S ARMY

said Abner unto him, Go, return. And he returned. **17** And Abner had communication with the elders of Israel, saying, Ye sought for David in times past to be king over you: **18** Now then do it: for the Lord hath spoken of David, saying, By the hand of my servant David I will save my people Israel out of the hand of the Philistines, and out of the hand of all their enemies. **19** And Abner also spake in the ears of Benjamin: and Abner went also to speak in the ears of David in Hebron all that seemed good to Israel, and that seemed good to the whole house of Benjamin. **20** So Abner came to David to Hebron, and twenty men with him. And David made Abner and the men that were with him a feast. **21** And Abner said unto David, I will arise and go, and will gather all Israel unto my lord the king, that they may make a league with thee, and that thou mayest reign over all that thine heart desireth. And David sent Abner away; and he went in peace.

Joab Kills Abner

22 And, behold, the servants of David and Joab came from pursuing a troop, and brought in a great spoil with them: but Abner was not with David in Hebron; for he had sent him away, and he was gone in peace. **23** When Joab and all the host that was with him were come, they told Joab, saying, Abner the son of Ner came to the king, and he hath sent him away, and he is gone in peace. **24** Then Joab came to the king, and said, What hast thou done? behold, Abner came unto thee; why is it that thou hast sent him away, and he is quite gone? **25** Thou knowest Abner the son of Ner, that he came to deceive thee, and to know thy going out and thy coming in, and to know all that thou doest. **26** And when Joab was come out from David, he sent messengers after Abner, which brought him again from the well of Sirah: but David knew it not. **27** And when Abner was returned to Hebron, Joab took him aside in the gate to speak with him *quietly, and smote him there under the fifth rib, that he died, for the blood of Asahel his brother. 28 And afterward when David heard it, he said, I and my kingdom are guiltless before the Lord for ever from the blood of Abner the son of Ner: 29 Let it rest on the head of Joab, and on all his father's house; and let there not fail from the house of Joab one that hath an issue, or that is a leper, or that leaneth on a staff, or that falleth on the sword, or that lacketh bread. 30 So Joab and Abishai his brother slew Abner, because he had slain their brother Asahel at Gibeon in the battle. 31 And David said to Joab, and to all the people that were with him, Rend your clothes, and gird you with sackcloth, and mourn before Abner. And king David himself followed the bier. 32 And they buried Abner in Hebron: and the king lifted up his voice, and wept at the grave of Abner; and all the people wept. 33 And the king lamented over Abner, and said, Died Abner as a fool dieth? 34 Thy hands were not bound, nor thy feet put into fetters: as a man falleth before wicked men, so fellest thou. And all the people wept again over him. 35 And when all the people came to cause David to eat meat while it was yet day, David sware, saying, So do God to me, and more also, if I taste bread, or ought else, till the sun be down. 36 And all the people took notice of it, and it pleased them: as whatsoever the king did pleased all the people. 37 For all the people and all Israel understood that day that it was not of the king to slay Abner the son of Ner. 38 And the king said unto his servants, Know ye not that there is a prince and a great man fallen this day in Israel? 39 And I am this day weak, though anointed king; and these men the sons of Zeruiah be too hard for me: the Lord shall reward the doer of evil according to his wickedness.*

Now, the opportunity had come when Abner visited David, as recorded in chapter 3 of 2nd Samuel. Abner came to David and was willing to turn over the kingdom of

JOAB, THE COMMANDER OF DAVID'S ARMY

Israel to David after supporting a son of Saul as king of Israel for two years. David, being the anointed one, was the rightful King of Israel and at this time Abner was ready to handover all of Israel to David.

Abner had a fruitful discussion with David on the issue of handing over all of Israel to David. David being a man with a large heart, forgave all the roles that Abner had played while he, David, had been a fugitive. He forgave him and recognized that Abner was a great warrior and one who would be useful to the kingdom of Israel. After their discussion, David bade Abner farewell without hurting him.

But that was not Joab's concern. All he was concerned about was avenging his brother's death. His whole being had been eaten up by resentment. When he came back and learnt that Abner had visited David and that he had let him go in peace, he was infuriated. He could not contain himself. How could such a thing happen?

He sent messengers to run after Abner and invite him back. Abner, suspecting nothing, having had such a wonderful meeting with the King, especially with the reassurance of the king that he was free to operate in the kingdom, honoured the request without question. And that was his undoing.

Joab took him and pretending to want a discussion, pierced him with his sword and killed him in cold blood. He killed him, not in warfare, but in an unguarded moment.

When King David heard about it, he wept. He was so upset that he lamented; "Why would you do this to a great warrior of Israel? Why would you waste blood like this?" David wailed for Abner's death. However, the fact remained that Abner was dead and Joab had obtained his revenge.

But you see, Joab must have thought that was the end. After all, he had gotten his revenge against Abner. Secondly, there wouldn't be the slightest opportunity for Abner to take away his position as the commander of the Israeli army under David. No. For him, Abner was dead and gone.

However, this was recorded against him in history, including what he did to Amasa, another great warrior of Israel. All these were results of the overwhelming spirit of vengeance and a wanton desire to put away anyone that seem to be a stumbling block to his remaining the commander of the Israeli army.

Like I had explained earlier, what unforgiveness does is to push one into exacting revenge. You may even get your vengeance and eventually achieve your desire to do something in retaliation but will that be the end of the story? Of course not! Rather, it is the beginning of the end.

That is exactly what happened to Joab. His actions

JOAB, THE COMMANDER OF DAVID'S ARMY

against Abner led to his death at the hand of Solomon.

1 Kings 2: 5 – 6, 28 – 34 (KJV)

[5] Moreover thou knowest also what Joab the son of Zeruiah did to me, and what he did to the two captains of the hosts of Israel, unto Abner the son of Ner, and unto Amasa the son of Jet her, whom he slew, and shed the blood of war in peace, and put the blood of war upon his girdle that was about his loins, and in his shoes that were on his feet. [6] Do therefore according to thy wisdom, and let not his hoar head go down to the grave in peace.

[28] Then tidings came to Joab: for Joab had turned after Adonijah, though he turned not after Absalom. And Joab fled unto the tabernacle of the LORD, and caught hold on the horns of the altar. [29] And it was told king Solomon that Joab was fled unto the tabernacle of the LORD; and, behold, he is by the altar. Then Solomon sent Benaiah the son of Jehoiada, saying, Go, fall upon him. [30] And Benaiah came to the tabernacle of the LORD, and said unto him, Thus saith the king, Come forth. And he said, Nay; but I will die here. And Benaiah brought the king word again, saying, Thus said Joab, and thus he answered me. [31] And the king said unto him, Do as he hath said, and fall upon him, and bury him; that thou mayest take away the innocent blood, which Joab shed, from me, and from the house of my father. [32] And the LORD shall return his blood upon his own head, who fell upon two men more righteous and better than he, and slew them with the sword, my father David not knowing thereof, to wit, Abner the son of Ner, captain of the host of Israel, and Amasa the son of Jether, captain of the host of Judah. [33] Their blood shall therefore return upon the head of Joab, and upon the head of his seed for ever: but upon David, and upon his seed, and upon his house, and upon his throne, shall there be peace for ever from the LORD. [34] So Benaiah the son

of Jehoiada went up, and fell upon him, and slew him: and he was buried in his own house in the wilderness.

In 1st Kings chapter 2 verses 5 to 6 and 28 to 34, on David's sick bed, he reminded Solomon not to forget the terrible acts of Joab against two great warriors of Israel. He added that Joab's grey hair should not go down to grave in peace. And of course, those actions of Joab became his waterloo and at the end of the day, he was also killed because of his actions against Abner and Amasa.

His end was a result of his actions against Abner and Amasa. That is it. Once you have avenged, you have planted the seed for your own destruction. Once you have avenged, that avenging becomes a seed planted for your own destruction; a path paved for your downfall.

That was how Joab was destroyed because he exacted vengeance against Abner and Amasa. Joab, the great commander of the Army of Israel under David, died a pitiable death and was remembered no more. His history was over. All the good works he had done were remembered no more. Instead, he was killed like a chicken and buried without fanfare. Such a man who had toiled and suffered for David, who had been ready to give his life for the life of David and who had expressed utmost loyalty for many years, died a pitiable death and all his efforts and deeds were remembered no more. Instead of being rewarded, he was now hunted. Instead of being exalted, he was rubbished and brought low.

That is exactly what an unforgiving spirit does to a man. It rubbishes him. It brings him down, makes him a non-entity and causes him to be forgotten by all. What men and women would remember about him would be that he was a terrible person because he had avenged a hurt to satisfy his resentment.

We are taking time to look at these cases so that we will see that there is nothing good in an unforgiving spirit. Absolutely nothing. It is bad on every side. It only brings one to a terrible and unsung end. It obliterates all our efforts and good deeds. It brings us to the point where we are only remembered for the evil that unforgiveness led us to.

May the Lord help us and give us a heart that is full of forgiveness. May the Lord enable us to live out what our Lord Jesus taught us to pray, "Father, forgive us as we forgive those who have erred against us." May the Lord grant us the grace, strength and power to live the life of forgiveness, forgiving one another even as He forgave us in Christ. May the Lord help us. This should be our prayer all the time: 'Lord, help me to live a life that is full of forgiveness'. Amen.

CHAPTER 8

AHITHOPHEL, DAVID'S COUNSELLOR
Felt Insulted by the Evil Action of Another

2 Samuel 11 (KJV)

David and Bath-sheba

11 And it came to pass, after the year was expired, at the time when kings go forth to battle, that David sent Joab, and his servants with him, and all Israel; and they destroyed the children of Ammon, and besieged Rabbah. But David tarried still at Jerusalem. 2 And it came to pass in an eveningtide, that David arose from off his bed, and walked upon the roof of the king's house: and from the roof he saw a woman washing herself; and the woman was very beautiful to look upon. 3 And David sent and enquired after the woman. And one said, Is not this Bathsheba, the daughter of Eliam, the wife of Uriah the Hittite? 4 And David sent messengers, and took her; and she came in unto him, and he lay with her; for she was purified from her uncleanness: and she returned unto her house. 5 And the woman conceived, and sent and told David, and said, I am with child. 6 And David sent to Joab, saying, Send me Uriah the Hittite. And Joab sent Uriah to David. 7 And when Uriah was come unto him, David demanded of him how Joab did, and how the people did, and how the war prospered. 8 And David said to Uriah, Go down to thy house, and wash thy feet. And Uriah departed out of the king's house, and there followed him a mess of meat from the king. 9 But Uriah slept at the door of the king's house with all the servants of his lord, and went not down to his house. 10 And when they had told David, saying,

AHITHOPHEL, DAVID'S COUNSELLOR

Uriah went not down unto his house, David said unto Uriah, Camest thou not from thy journey? why then didst thou not go down unto thine house? **11** And Uriah said unto David, The ark, and Israel, and Judah, abide in tents; and my lord Joab, and the servants of my lord, are encamped in the open fields; shall I then go into mine house, to eat and to drink, and to lie with my wife? as thou livest, and as thy soul liveth, I will not do this thing. **12** And David said to Uriah, Tarry here to day also, and to morrow I will let thee depart. So Uriah abode in Jerusalem that day, and the morrow. **13** And when David had called him, he did eat and drink before him; and he made him drunk: and at even he went out to lie on his bed with the servants of his lord, but went not down to his house. **14** And it came to pass in the morning, that David wrote a letter to Joab, and sent it by the hand of Uriah. **15** And he wrote in the letter, saying, Set ye Uriah in the forefront of the hottest battle, and retire ye from him, that he may be smitten, and die. **16** And it came to pass, when Joab observed the city, that he assigned Uriah unto a place where he knew that valiant men were. **17** And the men of the city went out, and fought with Joab: and there fell some of the people of the servants of David; and Uriah the Hittite died also. **18** Then Joab sent and told David all the things concerning the war; **19** And charged the messenger, saying, When thou hast made an end of telling the matters of the war unto the king, **20** And if so be that the king's wrath arise, and he say unto thee, Wherefore approached ye so nigh unto the city when ye did fight? knew ye not that they would shoot from the wall? **21** Who smote Abimelech the son of Jerubbesheth did not a woman cast a piece of a millstone upon him from the wall, that he died in Thebez? why went ye nigh the wall? then say thou, Thy servant Uriah the Hittite is dead also. **22** So the messenger went, and came and shewed David all that Joab had sent him for. **23** And the messenger said unto David, Surely the men prevailed against us, and came out unto us into the field, and we were upon *them even unto the entering of the gate. 24 And the shooters shot from off the wall upon thy servants; and some of the king's servants be dead, and thy servant Uriah the Hittite is dead also. 25 Then David said unto the messenger, Thus shalt thou say unto Joab, Let not this thing displease thee, for the sword devoureth one as well as another: make thy battle more strong against the city, and overthrow it: and encourage thou him. 26 And when the wife of Uriah heard that Uriah her husband was dead, she mourned for her husband. 27 And when the mourning was past, David sent and fetched her to his house, and she became his wife, and bare him a son. But the thing that David had done displeased the Lord.*

For a very long time, I have wondered how a man so close to David, who later became his most revered counsellor, could turn around to plot David's downfall and death. As the LORD helped me to see the reason for Ahithophel's action, I saw that if we allow bitterness to grow into an unforgiving spirit, we run the risk of sudden destruction by what I call the

Curse Of An Unforgiving Spirit.

In 2 Samuel 11:3 the Scripture says,
'So David sent and inquired about the woman. And some one said"Is this not Bathsheba, the daughter of Eliam, the wife of Uriah the Hittite?"'

In 2 Samuel 23:34, the Scripture while listing David's mighty men records, '...*Eliam the son of Ahithophel the Gilonite'.*

AHITHOPHEL, DAVID'S COUNSELLOR

The two verses above have established that Bathsheba, the daughter of Eliam and wife of Uriah the Hittite was the granddaughter of Ahithophel, David's most revered counsellor.

Bathsheba's father, Eliam being one of David's mighty men (2 Sam 23:34) must have been with David from his fugitive days when Saul drove David into hiding to the time he became Israel's king. He must have toiled for David and endangered his life to protect David.

Ahithophel, Bathsheba's grandfather (2 Sam 11:3; 23:34 and 15:12) was a man of the Law, religious and full of wisdom from above. He was David's counsellor and gave advice so accurate that it was regarded as the very 'oracle of God' (2 Sam 16: 23

> "And the counsel of Ahithophel, which he counselled in those days, was as if a man had enquired at the oracle of God: so was all the counsel of Ahithophel both with David and with Absalom". (KJV).)

He was the chief among David's counsellors and was highly regarded by David and all (I Chron. 27: 32 – 34).

> "32 Also Jonathan David's uncle was a counsellor, a wise man, and a scribe: and Jehiel the son of Hachmoni was with the king's sons: 33 And Ahithophel was the king's counsellor: and Hushai the Archite was the king's companion: 34 And after Ahithophel was Jehoiada the son of Benaiah, and Abiathar: and the general of the king's army was Joab". KJV).

Ahithophel, Eliam and by extension Bathsheba were all part of David's team right from the days he was living in caves and the woods as a fugitive. This family so gave themselves to the services of David that Ahithophel became the chief adviser while his son, Eliam was named among David's mighty men.

David's Sin: Adultery With Bathsheba (2 Sam 11: 1–5)

David committed adultery with Bathsheba, daughter of one of his mighty men, Eliam, and the granddaughter of his chief adviser and counsellor, Ahithophel.

Ahithophel, a man held in very high esteem, was a highly religious man who must have prided himself in the pious way he brought up members of his household. His fame was well known all over the country. This was the reason David and all who were with him were devastated when he joined Absalom's rebellion because he was the one man who could turn the battle against them with his oracle-like counsel.

David's adultery with Ahithophel's granddaughter must have devastated him. Ahithophel was a patriarch, a respected religious man, a teacher of the laws and an adviser par excellence. He could not believe that the family he built with so much zeal and pride could become an object of public ridicule and reduced to a family of shame in a nation that showed intolerance to adultery in an instant. In his time, a woman who commits adultery was killed by stoning with her family members casting the first stone in order to redeem their family honour. In this case, however, they could not because the king was involved.

Being betrayed by the one whom they esteemed and a friend and leader they have toiled for all their productive lives must have been a great shock to Ahithophel and his household. They had put their all in his service. Who would be in their shoes and not feel as terrible as they did? This act of betrayal by a loved one did not only shame Ahithophel, it also sowed in him a great seed of discord and a burning desire for revenge. And the societal status of the offender was not going to deter him.

David's closest adviser became his closest adversary without his knowledge. Although he was still in the king's employ, he was waiting for the right time to strike the king and exert vengeance for the shame and ridicule his family had been subjected to.

Every rational man, especially in Ahithophel's era and in consonance with the laws of the time, would most likely lend his full support to Ahithophel's rage and desire for revenge. He was hurt and disgraced by a beloved brother. However, because Ahithophel refused to come to terms with it, he allowed the dangerous seed of bitterness to be sown in his life. This bred a spirit that couldn't forgive and sought for a revenge that surpassed the crime committed against him.

A man of God, whose counsel was likened to God's Oracle, could not discern God's heart concerning the issue that was eating him up. He couldn't do this because what he perceived was done to him so outraged him that he became blind and deaf to whatsoever the Spirit of God was saying about the matter. The root of bitterness was formidable and brought him under the curse of an unforgiving spirit that eventually led to his self-destruction. Alas, a great man of God headed straight to the outer darkness to be tormented. (Mathew 18:34, 35

> " 34 And his lord was wroth, and delivered him to the tormentors, till he should pay all that was due unto him. 35 So likewise shall my heavenly Father do also unto you, if ye from your hearts forgive not everyone his brother their trespasses" KJV.)

Revenge: The Product Of An Unforgiving Spirit

Ahithophel's opportunity for revenge came when Absalom, David's son rebelled against his father, the king. 2 Sam.:15 12, 31

> " 12 And Absalom sent for Ahithophel the Gilonite, David's counsellor, from his city, even from Giloh, while he offered sacrifices. And the conspiracy was strong; for the people increased continually with Absalom, 31 And one told David, saying, Ahithophel is among the conspirators with Absalom. And David said, O LORD, I pray thee, turn the counsel of Ahithophel into foolishness." KJV

Two men with strong passion for revenge teamed up against David . When Absalom showed up against David,

AHITHOPHEL, DAVID'S COUNSELLOR

Ahithophel's delight knew no bounds. His first plan was to reduce the house of David to shame and public ridicule in order to exert a greater revenge. In 2 Sam.16: 20–23,

> "20 Then said Absalom to Ahithophel, Give counsel among you what we shall do. 21 And Ahithophel said unto Absalom, Go in unto thy father's concubines, which he hath left to keep the house; and all Israel shall hear that thou art abhorred of thy father: then shall the hands of all that are with thee be strong. 22 So they spread Absalom a tent upon the top of the house; and Absalom went in unto his father's concubines in the sight of all Israel. 23 And the counsel of Ahithophel, which he counselled in those days, was as if a man had enquired at the oracle of God: so was all the counsel of Ahithophel both with David and with Absalom" KJV

Ahithophel wrongly counselled Absalom to sleep with the concubines David left behind as he fled from Jerusalem and Absalom did this at the full glare of all Israel. David slept with Bathsheba in secret, but at the prodding of Ahithophel, Absalom slept with his father's concubines in public. The act was one so atrocious that it brought the house of David to public ridicule and shame. It made David's house a laughing stock. Sadly, although Ahithophel had avenged the wrong done against him on a higher dimension, he was not yet satisfied.

His next strategy was to bring a perpetual curse on the house of David. Ahithophel knew a person couldn't kill God's anointed without repercussions. He knew that whosoever killed God's anointed would bring a perpetual curse on his family.

I Sam.24: 5-7

" [5] *And it came to pass afterward, that David's heart smote him, because he had cut off Saul's skirt.* [6] *And he said unto his men, The* LORD *forbid that I should do this thing unto my master, the* LORD's *anointed, to stretch forth mine hand against him, seeing he is the anointed of the* LORD. [7] *So David stayed his servants with these words, and suffered them not to rise against Saul. But Saul rose up out of the cave, and went on his way".*

1 Sam. 26: 7-11

" [7] *So David and Abishai came to the people by night: and, behold, Saul lay sleeping within the trench, and his spear stuck in the ground at his bolster: but Abner and the people lay round about him.* [8] *Then said Abishai to David, God hath delivered thine enemy into thine hand this day: now therefore let me smite him, I pray thee, with the spear even to the earth at once, and I will not smite him the second time.* [9] *And David said to Abishai, Destroy him not: for who can stretch forth his hand against the* LORD's *anointed, and be guiltless?* [10] *David said furthermore, As the* LORD *liveth, the* LORD *shall smite him; or his day shall come to die; or he shall descend into battle, and perish.* [11] *The* LORD *forbid that I should stretch forth mine hand against the* LORD's *anointed: but, I pray thee, take thou now the spear that is at his bolster, and the cruse of water, and let us go.*

In order to annihilate the house of David and revoke God's covenant with David, Ahithophel advised Absalom to kill David, God's anointed and in so doing, incur the wrath of God on David's house. His plan was not just revenge but to cause the spiritual annihilation of David. His plan was perfect and he would have succeeded in aborting God's plan for the Messiah to come through David had God failed to intervene. In 2 Samuel 17: 1–14, verse 14 reads,

> 'So Absalom and all the men of Israel said "The advice of Hushai the Archite is better than the advice of Ahithophel" for the LORD had purposed to defeat the good advice of Ahithophel, to the intent that the LORD might bring disaster on Absalom".

From this, we can deduce that it was the LORD who delivered the house of David form a monumental disaster.

The Curse Of An Unforgiving Spirit

An unforgiving spirit is like cancer – it does not stop until it has consumed its victim. Ahithophel was not the only one grieved by David's action. God was also grieved as can be seen in 2 Samuel 11: 1 - 14 but God forgave David as he repented of his sin (Ps 51; 2 Sam.11: 13, 14). God in His mercy saw the heart of David and forgave him. However, Ahithophel, a man versed in God's ways refused to align himself with God and forgive as God forgave David but rather pursued his agenda for revenge. Regrettably, he destroyed himself for this reason. We may never know if Ahithophel thought his agenda of revenge was helping God punish David for his sin, but we do know that the outcome was suicide. 2 Sam. 17: 23

> *"23 And when Ahithophel saw that his counsel was not followed, he saddled his ass, and arose, and gat him home to*

his house, to his city, and put his household in order, and hanged himself, and died, and was buried in the sepulchre of his father".

He succeeded in killing himself in a shameful way and headed straight to hell. Surely, a spirit that fails to let go will end in the place of torment and unquenchable fire (Matt. 18: 34,35).

An Unforgiving Spirit Can Blind Us To God's Enduring Mercies

Is it not unfortunate how God in His infinite mercy will forgive our sin and yet someone holds on to the sin seeking to be His agent for meting our punishment? While Ahithophel was scheming and planning an appropriate punishment and shame for David and Bathsheba, God forgave them and moved on with His plan for mankind through them.

2 Samuel 12: 24,25

"²⁴ And David comforted Bathsheba his wife, and went in unto her, and lay with her: and she bare a son, and he called his name Solomon: and the LORD loved him. ²⁵ And he sent by the hand of Nathan the prophet; and he called his name Jedidiah, because of the LORD."

2 Samuel 12: 24-25 is very instructive of God's ways with His repentant children. David and Bathsheba repented of their grievous sin against God and He forgave them and gave them peace.

AHITHOPHEL, DAVID'S COUNSELLOR

The Bible in the above Scriptures says, 'Then David comforted Bathsheba, his wife, and went to her and lay with her. So she bore a son, and he called his name Solomon. Now the LORD loved him, and HE sent word by the hand of Nathan the prophet: So he called his name Jedidiah, because of the LORD'.

I want you to note this sentence in the scripture above: 'Now the LORD loved him, and HE sent word by the hand of Nathan the prophet...' Can the Lord be angry with a man He has forgiven and still love him to the extent that He sent his prophet to attend the naming ceremony of the man's child? Of course, it is not possible. The Lord had already forgiven them and that's why they had peace and could name their son Solomon, which means peace.

Even more, the LORD sent his prophet to name the child Jedidiah, which means beloved of God to confirm their peace with Him. The name shows God's love for Solomon as God had chosen him to be the successor to David's throne. This was a remarkable instance of God's goodness and grace considering the sinful nature of his parents' marriage. God did not stop there: both Mary and Joseph, the parents of our Lord Jesus Christ descended from Bathsheba, the wife of David. While Joseph descended through Solomon,

Matt. 1:6-16 (KJV)

"⁶ And Jesse begat David the king; and David the king begat Solomon of her that had been the wife of Urias; ⁷ And Solomon begat Roboam; and Roboam begat Abia; and Abia

begat Asa; [8] And Asa begat Josaphat; and Josaphat begat Joram; and Joram begat Ozias; [9] And Ozias begat Joatham; and Joatham begat Achaz; and Achaz begat Ezekias; [10] And Ezekias begat Manasses; and Manasses begat Amon; and Amon begat Josias; [11] And Josias begat Jechonias and his brethren, about the time they were carried away to Babylon: [12] And after they were brought to Babylon, Jechonias begat Salathiel; and Salathiel begat Zorobabel; [13] And Zorobabel begat Abiud; and Abiud begat Eliakim; and Eliakim begat Azor; [14] And Azor begat Sadoc; and Sadoc begat Achim; and Achim begat Eliud; [15] And Eliud begat Eleazar; and Eleazar begat Matthan; and Matthan begat Jacob; [16] And Jacob begat Joseph the husband of Mary, of whom was born Jesus, who is called Christ."

Mary descended through Nathan (Luke 3: 23 - 32)

"[23] And Jesus himself began to be about thirty years of age, being (as was supposed) the son of Joseph, which was the son of Heli, [24] Which was the son of Matthat, which was the son of Levi, which was the son of Melchi, which was the son of Janna, which was the son of Joseph, [25] Which was the son of Mattathias, which was the son of Amos, which was the son of Naum, which was the son of Esli, which was the son of Nagge, [26] Which was the son of Maath, which was the son of Mattathias, which was the son of Semei, which was the son of Joseph, which was the son of Juda, [27] Which was the son of Joanna, which was the son of Rhesa, which was the son of Zorobabel, which was the son of Salathiel, which was the son of Neri, [28] Which was the son of Melchi, which was the son of Addi, which was the son of Cosam, which was the son of Elmodam, which was the son of Er, [29] Which was the son of Jose, which was the son of Eliezer, which was the son of Jorim, which was the son of Matthat, which was the son of Levi, [30] Which was the son of Simeon, which was the son of Juda, which was the son of Joseph, which was the son of

Jonan, which was the son of Eliakim, [31]Which was the son of
Melea, which was the son of Menan, which was the son of
Mattatha, which was the son of Nathan, which was the son
of David, [32]Which was the son of Jesse, which was the son of
Obed, which was the son of Booz, which was the son of
Salmon, which was the son of Naasson,"KJV

Both sons of David came through Bathsheba (I Chron. 3: 1 -5).

"[1]Now these were the sons of David, which were born unto
him in Hebron; the firstborn Amnon, of Ahinoam the
Jezreelitess; the second Daniel, of Abigail the Carmelitess:
[2]The third, Absalom the son of Maachah the daughter of
Talmai king of Geshur: the fourth, Adonijah the son of
Haggith: [3]The fifth, Shephatiah of Abital: the sixth, Ithream
by Eglah his wife. [4]These six were born unto him in Hebron;
and there he reigned seven years and six months: and in
Jerusalem he reigned thirty and three years. [5]And these
were born unto him in Jerusalem; Shimea, and Shobab, and
Nathan, and Solomon, four, of Bathshua the daughter of
Ammiel" KJV

While David and Bathsheba were basking in God's
goodness, mercy and grace, Ahithophel was busy
planning deadly strategies to 'help' God punish these
sinners.

Is it not the same with many of us? We get offended by a
brother and the next thing we do is to play God. We
invest in planning strategies on how that 'very sinful'
brother should be dealt with. This is without prejudice to
the inner dealings of GOD and HIS son, whom you have

already written off. We get so eaten up by resentments, which in our blindness can lead us to self-destruction, while our Father has not only reconciled with His child but moved on to the next level with him.

CHAPTER 9

ABSALOM, SON OF DAVID
Accumulated Anger and Hatred over Perceived Inaction

Background

Absalom was the third son of David. He was one of the six sons David had while he ruled for seven and a half years in Hebron before he moved to Jerusalem as Israel's king. Absalom had issues that eventually cost him his life. He allowed an unforgiving spirit to eat into him and that eventually led to his death.

Absalom's problem can be traced to David's infidelity with Beersheba. That sin by David caused a lot of problems for his household – problems which moved on from one issue to another and eventually consumed Absalom.

Record has it that David's first son, Amnon had some unnatural desire for Tamar, his half-sister who was Absalom's sister. Amnon allowed himself to be deceived by Jehonadab, David's nephew. Jehonadab advised him to feign a sickness if he needed his half-sister so badly and in turn, request the King to send Tamar along to nurse him. So, Amnon did that.

Source Of His Offence

113

2 Samuel 13 (KJV)

1 And it came to pass after this, that Absalom the son of David had a fair sister, whose name was Tamar; and Amnon the son of David loved her. ² And Amnon was so vexed, that he fell sick for his sister Tamar; for she was a virgin; and Amnon thought it hard for him to do anything to her. ³ But Amnon had a friend, whose name was Jonadab, the son of Shimeah David's brother: and Jonadab was a very subtil man. ⁴ And he said unto him, Why art thou, being the king's son, lean from day to day? wilt thou not tell me? And Amnon said unto him, I love Tamar, my brother Absalom's sister. ⁵ And Jonadab said unto him, Lay thee down on thy bed, and make thyself sick: and when thy father cometh to see thee, say unto him, I pray thee, let my sister Tamar come, and give me meat, and dress the meat in my sight, that I may see it, and eat it at her hand. ¹⁰ And Amnon said unto Tamar, Bring the meat into the chamber, that I may eat of thine hand. And Tamar took the cakes which she had made, and brought them into the chamber to Amnon her brother. ¹¹ And when she had brought them unto him to eat, he took hold of her, and said unto her, Come lie with me, my sister. ¹² And she answered him, Nay, my brother, do not force me; for no such thing ought to be done in Israel: do not thou this folly. ¹³ And I, whither shall I cause my shame to go? and as for thee, thou shalt be as one of the fools in Israel. Now therefore, I pray thee, speak unto the king; for he will not withhold me from thee. ¹⁴ Howbeit he would not hearken unto her voice: but, being stronger than she, forced her, and lay with her. ¹⁵ Then Amnon hated her exceedingly; so that the hatred wherewith he hated her was greater than the love wherewith he had loved her. And Amnon said unto her, Arise, be gone. ¹⁶ And she said unto him, There is no cause: this evil in sending me away is greater than the other that thou didst unto me. But he would not hearken unto her. ¹⁷ Then he called his servant that ministered unto him, and said, Put now this woman out from me, and bolt the door after her. ¹⁸ And she had a

garment of divers colours upon her: for with such robes were the king's daughters that were virgins apparelled. Then his servant brought her out, and bolted the door after her. ¹⁹ *And Tamar put ashes on her head, and rent her garment of divers colours that was on her, and laid her hand on her head, and went on crying.* ²⁰ *And Absalom her brother said unto her, Hath Amnon thy brother been with thee? but hold now thy peace, my sister: he is thy brother; regard not this thing. So Tamar remained desolate in her brother Absalom's house.* ²¹ *But when king David heard of all these things, he was very wroth.* ²² *And Absalom spake unto his brother Amnon neither good nor bad: for Absalom hated Amnon, because he had forced his sister Tamar.*

Tamar obeyed her father's order to tend to Amnon and went to him bearing already prepared cakes and food. Prior to her arrival, Amnon had asked everyone in his vicinity to leave. When Tamar arrived, Amnon asked her to bring the food into his bedchamber and feed him herself. Tamar, believing her half-brother was sick, naïvely and out of care for him, took the cakes and food she prepared into his bedchamber. As Tamar approached Amnon, he grabbed her and demanded that she should sleep with him. Tamar resisted, telling him it is an abomination in Israel and would bring shame upon her. She insisted that this will bring Amnon down and make him a fool in Israel. She counselled him that if he wanted her so much, he could tell their father and have her as his wife.

However, Amnon, who at this time was overwhelmed by lust and possessed by the spirit of immorality, would not listen to Tamar. He raped her, took her virginity and disgraced her. After he had achieved his desire, he hated her. This same Tamar whom he had confessed so much love for, became nothing to him. The Bible said that he hated her with a hatred that was far greater than the love he had for her initially. Afterwards, he asked her to leave and when she hesitated, he called his servants to drive her out of his residence. Tamar was grieved and asked him not to do that as the sin of driving her out would be far greater than what he had just done. Amnon wouldn't listen and rather commanded his servants to push her out and lock the door against her. Her virginity taken from her, Tamar felt disgraced and tore her colourful dress that signified she was a virgin. She also put ashes on her head and put her hands on her head signifying she was mourning.

When David heard this, he was angry; however, the Bible has no record of any disciplinary action David meted out to Amnon. When Absalom got wind of what had transpired, he called his sister and pleaded with her to calm down, pleading with her that Amnon was her brother. Despite his efforts at peacemaking, Absalom did not speak to his half-brother, Amnon, as recorded in 2 Samuel 13:22. Why was this so? Absalom hated Amnon for forcing himself on his sister, Tamar and that was all it took to set the stage, sow the seed of bitterness and let an unforgiving spirit take over. Absalom refused to forgive Amnon. He nursed it in his heart and bided for time to exert his revenge on Amnon.

The Revenge

ABSALOM, SON OF DAVID

It took two whole years – two years of planning, two years of deceiving everyone that everything was okay before Absalom struck. He invited the sons of the king to his sheep shearing event. As they came and were merry and drinking, he instructed his servants to strike Amnon down and kill him as soon as he is merry and full of drink.

Absalom killed Amnon two years after Amnon had raped his sister and fled to Geshur, his mother's place for protection. He was away for three years in Gershur. Time went past but also afforded Absalom ample time to plan for further revenge as he was not yet done avenging the disgrace meted out to his sister, Tamar. The fact that the king did not take any decisive action against Amnon for defiling his sister made the king also culpable and deserving of some form of vengeance from Absalom. He was angry with his father for his inaction over the event and had decided not just to deal with Amnon but also with his father.

This situation of Absalom and David is prevalent today. So many people are angry with their fathers and mothers for what they did or did not do to them when they were growing up. In some cases, the hatred is so much that they will not want to have anything to do with their parents. Regrettably, they forget that this same people were the ones who brought them to this world. Some people are well-to-do now but their parents are languishing in poverty yet they care less; to them, their parents could as well be dead. Some people hold terrible grudges against their parents; some even wish that their parents were dead. What is more troubling and unfortunate is that a good number of these ones claim to be born again but they fail to realise that the same spirit that was at work in Absalom is at work in them today. Of course, the result of every unforgiving spirit is the same – destruction.

After three years, Absalom decided to come back to Jerusalem and David, unsuspecting of any evil, welcomed him. Absalom began by having his own courts, settling disputes and winning the support of the people of Israel. All these were part of his plan to undo his father because of the grudge he held. An unforgiving spirit can be terrible. David loved Absalom so much that he was unaware of his programmes and deadly plans to overthrow him as the King of Israel and eliminate him.

At the fullness of his plan, Absalom found an accomplice in Ahithophel, who also held terrible grudges against David for what David did to his granddaughter, Beersheba, the mother of Solomon. They came together and formulated a deadly plan fuelled by the grudges they held against David. Ahithophel who served as the chief counsellor of David before the Beersheba incident, became Absalom's chief counsellor. One of his early counsels to Absalom was to sleep with his father's concubines on top of the roof so that all of Israel will see and know that he is now in charge. This happened after David fled from Jerusalem because of Absalom's revolt. David slept with Beersheba in secret, but Ahithophel made the disgrace of David's concubines by his own son a public show. Ahithophel was riding on the back of Absalom's unforgiving spirit to exert his revenge not just on David but on his entire family. What he made Absalom do was an abomination that brought curses upon him and his lineage.

Their plan was to eliminate David and take over the kingship and with Absalom amassing a great number of soldiers with the help of Ahithophel, their plan was rock solid from a human perspective. However, because God was not with them, He confused them by using another friend of David, Hushai, to distort Ahithophel's counsel to Absalom. So, Absalom refused Ahithophel's seemingly great counsel and that led to Ahithophel's suicide. Taking the counter counsel of David's friend, Hushai, Absalom and his soldiers went in pursuit of David, with the intent of killing him and all his followers. He wanted to take over the kingship of Israel. Even so, David in his heart of love instructed that nobody should harm Absalom. His instruction was clear: fight the war and defeat Absalom but don't kill him. Absalom, on the other hand, was ready to kill his father and all that stood in his way of doing that. The rage in Absalom was so terrible that he decided to pursue his father and destroy him for a singular reason that had defined the events of his life.

His Death

2 Samuel Chapter 18 verses 9 to 18 (KJV)

⁹ And Absalom met the servants of David. And Absalom rode upon a mule, and the mule went under the thick boughs of a great oak, and his head caught hold of the oak, and he was taken up between the heaven and the earth; and the mule that was under him went away. ¹⁰ And a certain man saw it, and told Joab, and said, Behold, I saw Absalom hanged in an oak. ¹¹ And Joab said unto the man that told him, And, behold, thou sawest him, and why didst thou not smite him there to the ground? and I would have given thee ten shekels of silver, and a girdle. ¹² And the man said unto Joab, Though I should receive a thousand shekels of silver in mine hand, yet would I not put forth mine hand against the king's son: for in our hearing the king charged thee and Abishai and Ittai, saying, Beware that none touch the young man Absalom. ¹³ Otherwise I should have wrought falsehood against mine own life: for there is no matter hid from the king, and thou thyself wouldest have set thyself against me. ¹⁴ Then said Joab, I may not tarry thus with thee. And he took three darts in his hand, and thrust them through the heart of Absalom, while he was yet alive in the midst of the oak. ¹⁵ And ten young men that bare Joab's armour compassed about and smote Absalom, and slew him. ¹⁶ And Joab blew the trumpet, and the people returned from pursuing after Israel: for Joab held back the people. ¹⁷ And they took Absalom, and cast him into a great pit in the wood, and laid a very great heap of stones upon him: and all Israel fled every one to his tent. ¹⁸ Now Absalom in his lifetime had taken and reared up for himself a pillar, which is in the king's dale: for he said, I have no son to keep my name in remembrance: and he called the pillar after his own name: and it is called unto this day, Absalom's place.

The Bible records that as Absalom rode after his father and his soldiers in hot pursuit, his long hairs got entangled in the branch of a tree. That made him an easy prey for Joab, the commander of David's army and his soldiers, and they slaughtered him. That was Absalom's end. He died a shameful death and all those who were following him returned to their homes. In the end, David returned to Jerusalem as the king.

Lessons From Absalom

Absalom's story teaches us a lot. We can't neglect the lessons from the aftermath of the unforgiving spirit that possessed Absalom.

Indeed, it's really sad that we can hold on to hurts that were done to us by our parents for years on end. Even worse, we do not only hold on to them most times, we still desire to exert some form of revenge for those hurts. It's an unspoken truth that many people are languishing and devoid of progress in life because they still carry a lot of hatred and bitterness against their parents. You might have all the wealth in this world, but the question of how happy you are in it begs for answers. Have you sat back to consider the cause of the series of problems you've been passing through?

An unforgiving spirit is a cankerworm and even worse is one wielded against your parents. Irrespective of your parents' action against you, you must find a place in your heart to forgive them. They brought you to this world; the heights you have attained to were possible because they birthed you. Even if they misled or harmed you so badly, all you need to do is to lead a life that is worthy of emulation. You must love, bless and help your parents no matter their weaknesses. Failing to forgive your parents is a crime, one that has the ability to consume you if you do not let go of it.

Let us not be like Absalom; let's make a U-turn. Give your life to Christ and if you have given your life to Christ, then pray for your parents. If their ways are evil, pray that the Lord will touch and deliver them from such evil ways but don't hate them. Don't be bitter towards them; forgive them of all the wrongs they've done to you so that you will experience peace of mind and live long on this earth. **See Ephesians 6:1 – 3**. May the Lord help and save us from this unforgiving spirit that possessed Absalom.

Absalom so hated his brother to the point of killing him. Many a time, your siblings will hurt and do terrible things to you. Even so, you must forgive your siblings if you want to live a free life. Free yourself from the bondage of revenge and from the evil and curse of holding on to resentments by forgiving your siblings their errors and forgetting. You must forgive them completely. Help them if you are in a position to help irrespective of what they have done to you. Do this because a spirit that fails to let go will always breed destruction.

Regardless of who offended you, you will be on the path to destruction once you allow an unforgiving spirit eat into you. Release all those whom you've let your unforgiving spirit hold in captivity. Release them and be free in yourself so that the Lord may bless you and take care of you. Release them so you may reach your peak in life without destruction. You must rise above self-pity and this atrocious spirit that has nothing good in it for you. You must rise above it and allow the Lord heal your wounds and hurts Himself. Go to Him in prayer and plead with Him that you are sorry for letting an unforgiving spirit possess you for so long. Ask the Lord to grant you the grace and capacity to forgive. The Lord will surely do it for you. You will be able to forgive and experience a turnaround in your life because you have freed yourself from the curse of an unforgiving spirit.

CHAPTER 10

HAMAN THE AGAGITE
An Unforgiving Spirit As The Fruit Of Generational Hatred

(Esther 2:1, 10, 8:3, 5 ;(:24)

Haman has so elicited countless negative commentaries that even the reggae king, Bob Marley sang in one of his lyrics that 'he who digs a pit shall fall in it'. Haman is a classic example of God's sovereignty over all, especially His Sovereign purpose in protecting His own from all sorts of intrigues and devilish plans meant for His children's destruction.

However, one thing that has been lacking is a critical look at how Haman got to the sorry state he ended up in.
What was his motivation? What was eating him up? What exactly did he desire to achieve in annihilating the entire Jewish nation of his time? Why was he so passionate to the extent he was very willing to deplete his wealth considerably as long as he achieved his desire for the Jews. See:

Esther 3: 1 – 9 (KJV)

> *After these things did king Ahasuerus promote Haman the son of Hammedatha the Agagite, and advanced him, and set his seat above all the princes that were with him.[2] And all the king's servants, that were in the king's gate, bowed, and reverenced Haman: for the king had so commanded*

concerning him. But Mordecai bowed not, nor did him reverence. ³ Then the king's servants, which were in the king's gate, said unto Mordecai, Why transgressest thou the king's commandment? ⁴ Now it came to pass, when they spake daily unto him, and he hearkened not unto them, that they told Haman, to see whether Mordecai's matters would stand: for he had told them that he was a Jew. ⁵ And when Haman saw that Mordecai bowed not, nor did him reverence, then was Haman full of wrath. ⁶ And he thought scorn to lay hands on Mordecai alone; for they had shewed him the people of Mordecai: wherefore Haman sought to destroy all the Jews that were throughout the whole kingdom of Ahasuerus, even the people of Mordecai. ⁷ In the first month, that is, the month Nisan, in the twelfth year of king Ahasuerus, they cast Pur, that is, the lot, before Haman from day to day, and from month to month, to the twelfth month, that is, the month Adar. ⁸ And Haman said unto king Ahasuerus, There is a certain people scattered abroad and dispersed among the people in all the provinces of thy kingdom; and their laws are diverse from all people; neither keep they the king's laws: therefore it is not for the king's profit to suffer them. ⁹ If it please the king, let it be written that they may be destroyed: and I will pay ten thousand talents of silver to the hands of those that have the charge of the business, to bring it into the king's treasuries. "

To understand the source of Haman's burning passion to destroy all Jews, one needs to go beyond his time in order to piece together the source of his bitterness.

A spirit that fails to do away with grudges breeds a self-consuming fire, which though targeted at its object ends up in destroying the unforgiving one. This self-consuming fire is the CURSE that follows failing to let go.

The case of Haman the Agagite is a true picture of this self-destructive fire that follows a failure to forgive.

Before a person can appreciate the result or danger of not forgiving as depicted by Haman the Agagite, it is important we trace the historical antecedent that bred such unparalleled and deep rooted resentment towards the Jews in Haman.

Haman's lineage can be traced far back to Esau, son of Jacob. In Geneses 36:12 the Bible says,

> 'Now Timna was the concubine of Eliphaz the son of Adah, Esau's son, and she bore Amalek to Eliphaz...'

However, about 1000 years (1445BC) before the encounter of Haman and Mordecai, the Jews were attacked by the Amalekites when they left Egypt for the Promised Land.

Exodus 17:8-16 (KJV)
[8] Then came Amalek, and fought with Israel in Rephidim. [9] And Moses said unto Joshua, Choose us out men, and go out, fight with Amalek: to morrow I will stand on the top of the hill with the rod of God in mine hand. [10] So Joshua did as Moses had said to him, and fought with Amalek: and Moses, Aaron, and Hur went up to the top of the hill. [11] And it came to pass, when Moses held up his hand, that Israel prevailed: and when he let down his hand, Amalek prevailed. [12] But Moses hands were heavy; and they took a stone, and put it under him, and he sat thereon; and Aaron and Hur stayed up his hands, the one on the one side, and the other on the other side; and his hands were steady until the going down

of the sun. ¹³And Joshua discomfited Amalek and his people with the edge of the sword. ¹⁴And the LORD said unto Moses, Write this for a memorial in a book, and rehearse it in the ears of Joshua: for I will utterly put out the remembrance of Amalek from under heaven. ¹⁵And Moses built an altar, and called the name of it Jehovah nissi: ¹⁶For he said, Because the LORD hath sworn that the LORD will have war with Amalek from generation to generation

Consequent upon their dastardly act on the exiting Israelites, God pronounced a curse on the Amalekites, one which led to their obliteration from the earth.

Exodus 17:14, Deut 25:17-19. (KJV)

¹⁷Remember what Amalek did unto thee by the way, when ye were come forth out of Egypt; ¹⁸How he met thee by the way, and smote the hindmost of thee, even all that were feeble behind thee, when thou wast faint and weary; and he feared not God. ¹⁹Therefore it shall be, when the LORD thy God hath given thee rest from all thine enemies round about, in the land which the LORD thy God giveth thee for an inheritance to possess it, that thou shalt blot out the remembrance of Amalek from under heaven; thou shalt not forget it.

It is important to note that the Amalekites were not just descendants of Abraham, but proceeded from the loins of Isaac through a backslidden Esau. A bitter and backslidden child of God will easily be an agent of the devil in inflicting a most damaging wound on the Church if he is not restored.

Gen. 36: 12, 16 (KJV)

"¹²And Timna was concubine to Eliphaz Esau's son; and she bare to Eliphaz Amalek: these were the sons of Adah Esau's wife. ¹³And these are the sons of Reuel; Nahath, and Zerah, Shammah, and Mizzah: these were the sons of Bashemath Esau's wife. ¹⁴And these were the sons of Aholibamah, the daughter of Anah the daughter of Zibeon, Esau's wife: and she bare to Esau Jeush, and Jaalam, and Korah. ¹⁵These were dukes of the sons of Esau: the sons of Eliphaz the firstborn son of Esau; duke Teman, duke Omar, duke Zepho, duke Kenaz, ¹⁶Duke Korah, duke Gatam, and duke Amalek: these are the dukes that came of Eliphaz in the land of Edom; these were the sons of Adah."

The Amalekites had always desired the destruction of Israel either in confederacy with other nations or in pursuit of Israel for harm. See:

Psalm 83: 1 – 8 (KJV) –

Amalekites in confederacy to destroy Israel

1 Keep not thou silence, O God: hold not thy peace, and be not still, O God. ²For, lo, thine enemies make a tumult: and they that hate thee have lifted up the head. ³They have taken crafty counsel against thy people, and consulted against thy hidden ones. ⁴They have said, Come, and let us cut them off from being a nation; that the name of Israel may be no more in remembrance. ⁵For they have consulted together with one consent: they are confederate against thee: ⁶The tabernacles of Edom, and the Ishmaelites; of Moab, and the Hagarenes; ⁷Gebal, and Ammon, and Amalek; the Philistines with the inhabitants of Tyre; ⁸Assur also is joined with them: they have holpen the children of Lot. Selah.

HAMAN THE AGAGITE

Ex.17:8 -13 – (KJV)

In war with Israel during Israel's Exodus from Egypt;

"*8 Then came Amalek, and fought with Israel in Rephidim. 9 And Moses said unto Joshua, Choose us out men, and go out, fight with Amalek: to morrow I will stand on the top of the hill with the rod of God in mine hand. 10 So Joshua did as Moses had said to him, and fought with Amalek: and Moses, Aaron, and Hur went up to the top of the hill. 11 And it came to pass, when Moses held up his hand, that Israel prevailed: and when he let down his hand, Amalek prevailed. 12 But Moses hands were heavy; and they took a stone, and put it under him, and he sat thereon; and Aaron and Hur stayed up his hands, the one on the one side, and the other on the other side; and his hands were steady until the going down of the sun. 13 And Joshua discomfited Amalek and his people with the edge of the sword.*" KJV

Judge 6: 3 - 6 (KJV)

In collaboration with the Midianites to destroy the livelihood of the Israelites

"*3 And so it was, when Israel had sown, that the Midianites came up, and the Amalekites, and the children of the east, even they came up against them; 4 And they encamped against them, and destroyed the increase of the earth, till thou come unto Gaza, and left no sustenance for Israel, neither sheep, nor ox, nor ass. 5 For they came up with their cattle and their tents, and they came as grasshoppers for multitude; for both they and their camels were without number: and they entered into the land to destroy it. 6 And Israel was greatly impoverished because of the Midianites; and the children of Israel cried unto the LORD.*

1 Sam 15: 1 – 8 (KJV)

God ordered the obliteration of Amalekites because of their wickedness towards Israel

> "¹Samuel also said unto Saul, The LORD sent me to anoint thee to be king over his people, over Israel: now therefore hearken thou unto the voice of the words of the LORD. ² Thus saith the LORD of hosts, I remember that which Amalek did to Israel, how he laid wait for him in the way, when he came up from Egypt. ³ Now go and smite Amalek, and utterly destroy all that they have, and spare them not; but slay both man and woman, infant and suckling, ox and sheep, camel and ass. ⁴ And Saul gathered the people together, and numbered them in Telaim, two hundred thousand footmen, and ten thousand men of Judah. ⁵ And Saul came to a city of Amalek, and laid wait in the valley. ⁶ And Saul said unto the Kenites, Go, depart, get you down from among the Amalekites, lest I destroy you with them: for ye shewed kindness to all the children of Israel, when they came up out of Egypt. So the Kenites departed from among the Amalekites. ⁷ And Saul smote the Amalekites from Havilah until thou comest to Shur, that is over against Egypt. ⁸ And he took Agag the king of the Amalekites alive, and utterly destroyed all the people with the edge of the sword.

Although God commanded Saul at about 1030 BC to completely eliminate the Amalekites including their King Agag (1 Sam 15:2,3), Saul a Benjamite disobeyed the order (1 Sam 15:7-9) (1Sam 15:11,26;28:18). Samuel finally carried out God's order by cutting king Agag into pieces. Samuel although a Levite, had his home in Ramah, a hill country in the tribe of Benjamin.

HAMAN THE AGAGITE

Haman the Agagite came from the lineage of king Agag and though Esther arrived about 550 years after the death of King Agag, Haman still bore a deep rooted animosity against the Jews in spite of the time that had passed. Like Ahithophel, he was bidding his time while planning for sweet revenge. His plan was to annihilate the Jews thereby avenging to some degree, what the Jews did to his people. The fact that Mordecai was a Benjamite and King Saul's and Prophet Samuel's kinsmen compounded his hatred.

This explains why Haman so viciously attempted to exterminate the Jewish race (Esther 3:5, 6, 13) and would have succeeded if not for God.

This burning desire for revenge resulted from an inherited generational root of bitterness. His unforgiving spirit led to his destruction by the fanned embers of the fire of resentment ignited in him. The gallows he built for Mordecai was where he was hanged. The thirteenth day of the month Adar that he choose and got permission from king Ahassaurus for the elimination of the Jews became the day his ten sons were hanged and all his followers killed by rampaging and empowered Jews.

See Esther 7: 6 – 10 (KJV)

Haman Is Hanged

> [6] And Esther said, [†]The adversary and enemy is this wicked Haman. Then Haman [d]was afraid [||]before the king and the queen. [7] And the king arising from the banquet of wine in his

wrath went into *the palace garden: and Haman stood up to make request for his life to Esther the queen; for he saw that there was *evil determined against him by the *king. *Then the king returned out of *the palace garden into the place of the banquet of wine; and Haman was fallen upon *the bed whereon Esther was. Then said the king, Will he force the queen also *before me in the house? As the word went out of the king's mouth, they covered Haman's face. *And *Harbonah, one of the chamberlains, said before the king, Behold also, the *gallows fifty cubits high, which Haman had made for Mordecai, *who had spoken good for the king, standeth in the house of Haman. Then the king said, Hang him thereon. *So they hanged Haman on the gallows that he had prepared for Mordecai. Then *was the king's wrath pacified.

See also Esther 9: 10 – 17 (KJV)

Haman's ten sons and collaborators are killed

10 The ten sons of Haman the son of Hammedatha, the enemy of the Jews, slew they; but on the spoil laid they not their hand.11 On that day the number of those that were slain in Shushan the palace was brought before the king.12 And the king said unto Esther the queen, The Jews have slain and destroyed five hundred men in Shushan the palace, and the ten sons of Haman; what have they done in the rest of the king's provinces? now what is thy petition? and it shall be granted thee: or what is thy request further? and it shall be done.13 Then said Esther, If it please the king, let it be granted to the Jews which are in Shushan to do to morrow also according unto this day's decree, and let Haman's ten sons be hanged upon the gallows.14 And the king commanded it so to be done: and the decree was given at Shushan; and they hanged Haman's ten sons.15 For the Jews that were in Shushan gathered themselves together on the fourteenth day also of the month Adar, and slew three

*hundred men at Shushan; but on the prey they laid not their hand.***16** *But the other Jews that were in the king's provinces gathered themselves together, and stood for their lives, and had rest from their enemies, and slew of their foes seventy and five thousand, but they laid not their hands on the prey,***17** *On the thirteenth day of the month Adar; and on the fourteenth day of the same rested they, and made it a day of feasting and gladness.*

It is easy to let the spirit of generational or family animosities towards a race, family or person fan in us embers of a self-consuming fire especially when the target of our grudges and desire for revenge is GOD's child or people.

Beware! Beware! Beware!

CHAPTER 11

JONAH THE PROPHET

Angry Over God's Goodness To Those He Desired Punished

"Now the LORD had prepared a great fish to swallow up Jonah. And Jonah was in the belly of the fish three days and three nights." (Jonah 1:17.) KJV

Jonah the prophet was sent by God to Nineveh. Even so, a little background information may be very necessary. According to

2nd Kings 14:25

> ²⁵ He restored the coast of Israel from the entering of Hamath unto the sea of the plain, according to the word of the LORD God of Israel, which he spake by the hand of his servant Jonah, the son of Amittai, the prophet, which was of Gathhepher.

Jonah came from Gathhepher near Nazareth. That placed him as a prophet that reigned around the time of Jeroboam the second that should be between 793 and 753 BC, making him a prophet that God raised to the northern tribes of Israel, the 10 tribes of the north of Israel.

Jonah was sent to Nineveh, which at a time was the capital of Assyria. It probably was the richest and most prosperous city in the world because it was the capital of

JONAH THE PROPHET

Assyria when Assyria held sway over most parts of the world. Jonah, however, refused to carry out God's mandate for him to preach against the prevailing wickedness in Nineveh.

Jonah 1:1 - 4

> [1] Now the word of the LORD came unto Jonah the son of Amittai, saying, Arise, go to Nineveh, that great city, and cry against it; for their wickedness is come up before me. [3] But Jonah rose up to flee unto Tarshish from the presence of the LORD, and went down to Joppa; and he found a ship going to Tarshish: so he paid the fare thereof, and went down into it, to go with them unto Tarshish from the presence of the LORD. [4] But the LORD sent out a great wind into the sea, and there was a mighty tempest in the sea, so that the ship was like to be broken.

God's intent was for Nineveh to hear the Gospel and repent from their wickedness.

Jonah was a typical Jew who hated the guts of the Assyrians because they oppressed the Jews. Assyrians have been in perpetual enmity with the Jews. They ransacked the northern tribes and did all manner of evil to Israel.

> [4] For thus saith the Lord GOD, My people went down aforetime into Egypt to sojourn there; and the Assyrian oppressed them without cause. (Isaiah 52:4) KJV

And here was a man, a true Israelite, a prophet in Israel asked by God to go and preach to Nineveh, the capital of a nation that hated Israel so much. A man asked to preach so they may repent and turn from their wickedness and be saved from God's punishment and judgment.

Of course as a true Jew, who did not want to see any good except God's judgment and punishment on Assyria that was a task too much for Jonah to carry out. It was a tall task. He would have preferred that God would punish and judge Nineveh so harshly if for no other reason but to avenge all the wickedness and oppression of Nineveh on Israel.

This is simply the workings of man. A man that is filled with resentments will always desire for some sort of mishap to happen to the one whom he bears grudges against.

Jonah could not see himself forgiving the Assyrians or her capital, Nineveh for all the evil that they did to Israel. As a result, he felt being asked to be an instrument and agent for averting punishment or judgment upon Nineveh or Assyria was unthinkable. He could not comprehend it and was not ready even as a prophet of God to do His bidding.

Instead of going to Nineveh to preach against her wickedness as commanded by God, Jonah arose to flee to Tarshish. He tried to run away from the presence of God and he went to Joppa. He found a ship going to Tarshish, paid for the fare and boarded it. It is sad that a prophet of his calibre could believe that God's Hand would not reach him in Tashish. The Psalmist in **Psalm 139** was explicit in his assertion that there is no hiding place from God.

> [1] O lord, thou hast searched me, and known me. [2] Thou knowest my downsitting and mine uprising, thou understandest my thought afar off. [3] Thou compassest my path and my lying down, and art acquainted with all my ways. [4] For there is not a word in my tongue, but, lo, O LORD, thou knowest it altogether. [5] Thou hast beset me behind and before, and laid thine hand upon me. [6] Such knowledge is too wonderful for me; it is high, I cannot attain unto it. [7] Whither shall I go from thy spirit? or whither shall I flee from thy presence? [8] If I ascend up into heaven, thou art there: if I make my bed in hell, behold, thou art there. [9] If I take the wings of the morning, and dwell in the uttermost parts of the sea; [10] Even there shall thy hand lead me, and thy right hand shall hold me. [11] If I say, Surely the darkness shall cover me; even the night shall be light about me. [12] Yea, the darkness hideth not from thee; but the night shineth as the day: the darkness and the light are both alike to thee (Psalm 139: 1 – 12) KJV

Many of us especially God's children occasionally behave as if God is far from us and as if we can hide our deeds from His presence. It is not possible at all. The Lord is everywhere.

Jonah was so carried away by his anger and bitterness that he behaved as if God was not even in the ship he had boarded – as if God was not in the ocean that the ship will sail on, as if God was not everywhere. This was a prophet who should have known better. His behaviour and seeming forgetfulness of the attributes of the God he served was simply the outcome of suppressed hurts.

THE FRUIT OF UNFORGIVENESS

When we allow the fruit of bitterness and generational unforgiving spirit to overwhelm us, it causes us to lose our sense of reason and everything that is good in us. It makes our whole system become so bitter that we entertain irrational thoughts and actions. This was Jonah's problem.

Nevertheless, God was insistent on Jonah carrying out His commands, so Jonah had to end up in the belly of the fish for three days. It took his sojourn in the belly of the fish for him to repent of his folly. After the encounter, he was now willing to do God's biding. The fish at the behest of God, spewed him out and he preached in Nineveh. At his preaching, everyone in the great city of Nineveh, from the King to the peasants repented. There was a decree and there was fasting and thorough repentance by the people from their wickedness. And God showed mercy on them for their repentance.

In chapter 4 of the book of Jonah, Jonah became so angry that God pardoned the people of Nineveh. He prayed to the Lord saying 'Ah Lord! was not this what I said when I was still in my country, therefore I fled previously to Tashish, for I know that You are a gracious and merciful God, slow to anger and abundant in loving kindness, one who relents from doing harm, therefore now Oh Lord, please take my life from me, for it is better for me to die than to live.'

¹But it displeased Jonah exceedingly, and he was very angry.
² And he prayed unto the LORD, and said, I pray thee, O LORD,

was not this my saying, when I was yet in my country? Therefore I fled before unto Tarshish: for I knew that thou art a gracious God, and merciful, slow to anger, and of great kindness, and repentest thee of the evil. ³ Therefore now, O LORD, take, I beseech thee, my life from me; for it is better for me to die than to live. ⁴ Then said the LORD, Doest thou well to be angry? (Jonah 4: 1 – 4) KJV

It was better for him to die than to live and see God's graciousness on the people of Nineveh. His resentment had eaten into him so badly that he would prefer to die than to see good come upon the people his whole being had such a root of bitterness against because of past hurts.

An unforgiving spirit builds a route of bitterness that transcends every aspect of our being and encapsulates us into a tight corner with a system full of gall of bitterness. Sadly, this yields nothing but destruction. We see Jonah demand to die rather than to see this people repent and be forgiven by God. It is important for us to know the Heart of God. In this account, God desired that the people of Nineveh would repent and taste of His mercy and grace. And in their repentance, God graciously forgave them and showered His mercy all over them.

It took another one hundred and fifty years for Nineveh to be destroyed after they repented as a result of Jonah's preaching. However, Jonah couldn't rejoice that a whole nation repented through his ministry and came to God. He was not keen on the beauty of what God had done through him. He was embittered and desired to die rather than see the goodness of God expressed to his perceived enemies The salvation of Nineveh during Jonah's time should mean a decoration of stars and stars upon his crown. According to Daniel 12:3, those who bring men to God shall shine as stars.

> [3] And they that be wise shall shine as the brightness of the firmament; and they that turn many to righteousness as the stars forever and ever **(Daniel 12:3) KJV**

.

It is important for us to yield to God and let Him clean us thoroughly from every root of bitterness and unforgiving spirit. We must pray that God will give us the mind of Christ – the mind that forgave while suffering on the cross. That is the mind that is acceptable to God and what we need. Christ did so much for us. Why can't we in the same vein replicate a little to those who have wronged us or our loved ones? Let us not be like Jonah. Let us walk with God who has commanded us to love our enemies and give water to those who persecute us. Let us love those who hate us and do good to them. God's mercy may reach them due to our actions and they will become our brothers as they come into God's kingdom. And that will be the beautiful stars on our Crown.

Let us desire that by the love and forgiveness we show towards those who have wronged us or our loved ones, they will come to know the saving grace of our Lord and master Jesus Christ. There is nothing as beautiful and wonderful as this. Your act of forgiveness can bring someone who has wronged you so badly, that is even so scared of coming near you, to Christ. It can also cause a new change in his way of living.

Let us give the Lord a chance in us, to heal us of every wrong and unforgiving spirit. Let's give Him the chance to heal us completely and use us as agents, like Jonah, in bringing our oppressors to God through Christ our Lord. Amen.

CHAPTER 12

AN UNFORGIVING SPIRIT IN THE HOME FRONT

At The Beginning...

When we fall in love, we go all out to express our love to the one we love. During our courtship period, there is hardly any negative information about our loved one that means a thing to us. We rebuff our parents, friends, relatives and others to cling tightly to the one we love. Some of us go to the extent of saying that we would not marry any other person except the one we have chosen. We call the person countless sweet names; names like 'my sweetheart', 'the sugar in my tea', 'sweetest honey', 'my best friend', 'the one that makes my heart smile,' amongst others. We seldom stay one day without seeing the person and would always bombard them with phone calls and messages several times a day.

Then we marry them and everything gradually begins to change. After two or three years, it all fades off. The angel becomes a witch; the one you declared as the only one who can share your future now turns out to be the hindrance to the good things in your future. Unprintable names replace all those sweet names.

The day of marriage revolves around the bridegroom and bride. The man is the bridegroom – the groom of the bride. A woman is a raw material given to the man on his wedding day to groom. She is given to the man so he can produce someone that is beautiful in character and lifestyle, someone who will continually excite him. It is therefore the duty of the man, who now becomes a co-worker with the Manufacturer (God), to groom this woman so she can become who he wants her to be.

This means that, if after four, five or ten years, this angel (according to you on your wedding day) who should be groomed to an archangel becomes a witch instead (according to your latest definition of her), you have failed woefully in your grooming duty. What she has become is what you have made out of her. If she becomes antagonistic, nagging, unbearable, and all the unprintable names you call her, it means that those are what you have made out of her. Those are the outcome of your grooming activities.

If your wife fails to meet your standard and needs, the truth is there for all to see: you are the one who has failed woefully in your grooming duty as a husband. The man has a great responsibility – the responsibility of grooming. That is why you should not destroy your wife for not meeting your expectations or allow an unforgiving spirit overwhelm you because you are the bridegroom.
The husband's key assignment is to nurture, nourish and cherish his wife as Christ loved the Church. Ephesians 5 Verse 28 is very instructive,

[28] So ought men to love their wives as their own bodies. He that loveth his wife loveth himself'.

You do yourself a favour when you love and take care of your wife. From this scripture, you are what you call your wife. If you call her a witch or a bitch, that's what you made out of her and I am afraid you are also the same thing you think she is.

There should be no room for hatred, rancour and venom in your home. There should be no place for name calling in your home. The sweetness of your courtship days can be experienced again in your home if you will hand over your marriage completely to God for safe keeping. We should look back, sit down and ask God to bring us into what He desires for us to be.

An unforgiving spirit in marriage

Many marriages are in turmoil today because the husband and wife have hurt against each other and allowed the hurt grow till it became a giant inside of them. The hurt becomes a terrible unforgiving spirit, which they hold on to tenaciously. Some spouses let the hurts fester to the point that nothing their wife or husband does pleases them. Eventually, this eats up the fabric of the marriage and the home becomes chaotic while both partners live like flatmates.

I managed a case of what an unforgiving spirit can do to a marriage when I was pastoring a church in Nigeria. It was a terrible experience. I had been called in by the head of the denomination I was pastoring to urgently visit the home of a member of the congregation I was pastoring. We were told that the husband was about to kill his wife. My wife and I entered the car and got to the home. When we arrived, two other pastors and their wives were already there. It was a messy situation.

This brother had a machete in hand. Fortunately, the wife was able to wrest the machete off his hands. We were amazed at the development and tried to inquire from the brother what really went wrong, he opened up and shared what happened when they were courting. He and his wife were both students and their schools were about 300 kilometres apart. One day, he travelled from his school to the sister's school to visit his love. During the visit, he slept over and they committed fornication which led to a pregnancy for which he had to marry her.

From the brother's story, we were able to deduce that he believed the sister deceived him into committing fornication with her. This sounded absurd since he was the one who travelled over 300 kilometres to visit a single lady in her school. This fighting incident happened twelve years after the primary incident. And for those twelve years, he nursed grudges against his wife for making him sleep with her before their marriage. He could not trust her anymore; whosoever she greets on the way is her boyfriend and sleeping partner. The marriage was in ruins because he could not forgive himself for falling for the sister's 'deceit' according to him. Twelve years after and there was still animosity. The joy of the Lord was lost and there was no Christian home in place. The only child of the marriage at the time, the product of the incident, lived in a home where love was missing and respect for the mother of the home, gone.

The brother maintained that before the incident, he was a virgin. But the question of how he could say that he was lured into fornication when he actually travelled a far distance alone to visit a single lady, his girlfriend, was one that made his assertion funny. I wondered what he expected when he made the trip himself. Yet, he was telling the world that she lured him into sin while painting himself as the righteous one and his wife as the embodiment of Satan. He hated her for that reason. It became difficult for him to forgive her because he had not been able to forgive himself for giving in to the act of fornication. His wife suffered untold hardship in his home because he did not have the capacity to forgive himself for falling prey to the sin of fornication and therefore, it became impossible for him to forgive his fornicating mate.

This is very sad and a problem that is plaguing many homes. In so many families, a good number of husbands have hurts they hold so strongly in their hearts against their wives. Same can be said of many wives. In some cases, the other party may have had some failures, which would give them something to lay hold on. So, a partner may look for an excuse to hold the other partner in resentment for their failure because they have not been able to forgive themselves for it.

AN UNFORGIVING SPIRIT IN THE HOME FRONT

This would bring tumult to the home and the children will experience nothing but series of problems. Nothing would move smoothly; the children would be exposed to a fake life. Stagnation is found all over the place because an unforgiving spirit lies underneath. The home would become full of unhappiness and the gall of bitterness would overtake the souls and emotions of the ones living in such a home.

When Things Go Sour...

If you have a problem as a bridegroom, you have the main Manufacturer, God, who can help you realise what He wants out of your wife, which will undoubtedly be pleasing and helpful to you. God has made her your helpmate and it is through God and by Him that you will help her become what you want her to be. God is the medium who will help your wife come forth as gold that is fit as your helpmate. Don't rely on human methods in your grooming or the grooming work will be abysmal and eat you up. The effect will make the angel you married seem like an alien.

That is why you must always seek the help of the Master Builder in building your spouse into a person who is pleasing to God because anyone who is pleasing to God will definitely meet your needs. Rather than destroying this woman whom God has given to you, sit back and deal with your failures and inabilities. Sit back and ask God to help you forgive yourself for having failed so woefully in the grooming assignment that He gave to you. Repent of your failures. Ask the Lord to forgive you and help you forgive yourself. Ask Him to endow you with the capacity to forgive your wife and to enrich your wife with a large heart to forgive all the wickedness you have perpetrated against her. Ask God to grant you wisdom to carry on effectively with your grooming assignment. Allow the power of the Almighty God through our Lord Jesus Christ who loves you so much, work out grooming results that will amaze you. A very instructive scripture is Ephesians 5: 22-35 (KJV):

> [22] *Wives, submit yourselves unto your own husbands, as unto the Lord.* [23] *For the husband is the head of the wife, even as Christ is the head of the church: and he is the saviour of the body.* [24] *Therefore as the church is subject unto Christ, so let the wives be to their own husbands in every thing.* [25] *Husbands, love your wives, even as Christ also loved the church, and gave himself for it;* [26] *That he might sanctify and cleanse it with the washing of water by the word,* [27] *That he might present it to himself a glorious church, not having spot, or wrinkle, or any such thing; but that it should be holy and without blemish.* [28] *So ought men to love their wives as their own bodies. He that loveth his wife loveth himself.* [29] *For no man ever yet hated his own flesh; but nourisheth and cherisheth it, even as the Lord the church:* [30] *For we are members of his body, of his flesh, and of his bones.* [31] *For this cause shall a man leave his father and mother, and shall be joined unto his wife, and they two shall be one flesh.* [32] *This is a great mystery: but I speak concerning Christ and the church.* [33] *Nevertheless let every one of you in particular so love his wife even as himself; and the wife see that she reverence her husband.*

AN UNFORGIVING SPIRIT IN THE HOME FRONT

Like the Lord warned Cain of how dangerous the path he was taking was and how he would be better if he turned back, He is speaking to you as a married person. Those people who are advising and insisting you exert your revenge are the ones killing you. They are your real enemies and are helping you dig your own grave. They are leading you to an early grave – to a life of unhappiness, sadness, bitterness and hatred.

No road exists along that way you're going. So, it is better you make a U-turn and discard such people because they are enemies of your soul. Discard them and return to your senses. Kneel by your bedside, cry to God, tell Him you are sorry and ask Him to forgive you. Ask Him to grant you the grace to forgive yourself and the capacity to forgive your partner.

Once you do this, a new kind of joy will flood your life. You will be able to forgive yourself and your partner. A new healing will flow into your marriage through this flood of forgiveness. This will usher in newness of life to your marriage – new gladness, new happiness and a home filled with joy and life. Instead of death, life will come. However, when you continue pursuing a life filled with resentment, you will bring death upon not just your marriage, but your life.

I urge you to save your marriage by loving and forgiving your spouse from the bottom of your heart. Learn to forgive yourself for your failures – only then will it be easier for you to forgive your spouse for his/her failures.

THE FRUIT OF UNFORGIVENESS

Forgive your spouse for whatsoever you may think she or he has done to you and bring back life into your marriage and home.

Similarly, many people today are living lives of misery because of the unsavoury baggage of an unforgiving spirit that they carry about them against their parents or siblings. Any mention or thoughts of their parents or siblings overwhelms them with hatred, bitterness and venom. This unleashes a cloud of sadness over them. It is a torture, not on the one they are bitter about, but on themselves.

This is why many who are living under such bondage easily become patients of terrible ailments. It also impedes their spiritual growth as it becomes a cloud hindering their prayers and intimate fellowship with God. So apart from being a spiritual no-no, an unforgiving spirit has adverse effect on one's health. This makes seeking timely solution from the curse inherent in not forgiving your parents and siblings a necessity. You must seek God's forgiveness for harbouring resentment towards your parents or your siblings and consequently, making light of Christ forgiveness of your sins.

Do yourself a favour and be set free from this destructive spirit. It is really important that we sit back, check ourselves and see if there is anyone we are holding hostage, especially our parents, our siblings or our relatives. They may have offended us, caused us some untold pains and taken advantage of us but still we have to, for our good, let go and forgive them. An unforgiving spirit breeds all manner of ailments – high blood pressure, ulcer, anxiety and the likes. Even worse, nothing can be more terrible than seeing the person you are bearing such terrible grudges against and having your whole system upset.

Let go and be free. Let go of the pains. Your parents brought you into this world. Let the hurts go irrespective of what they have done to wrong you. Release your siblings; they may have mocked you or wronged you badly, but letting go does you good. An unforgiving spirit only leads one to self-destruction. The time and effort you put into your plan to avenge will do you no good. Do yourself a great favour and forgive them even as Christ forgave you. Release them as Christ released you. Save yourself from unnecessary evil, release them and free yourself.

Choose life today and discard the unforgiving spirit. Seek the Lord's forgiveness and pray that He will increase your capacity to forgive your partner and even forgive those enemies who disguised as friends and misled you. The Lord wishes to grant us the kingdom and all it contains: happiness, joy, goodness, love, kindness and abundant grace. Good things abound in the kingdom; an unforgiving spirit, hatred, bitterness and malice aren't dividends of the kingdom.

You must ask the Lord to forgive you and give you back the kingdom. Give your marriage back to the kingdom.

Praise the Lord – He is willing. May He grant us the willingness to accept our need of Him and break free of any unforgiving spirit. May He save us from all forms of bitterness, malice and hatred. May the Lord have mercy on us. Amen.

SECTION TWO
The Cure

CHAPTER 13

DEALING WITH AN UNFORGIVING SPIRIT

Matthew 18 (KJV)

1 At the same time came the disciples unto Jesus, saying, Who is the greatest in the kingdom of heaven? ² And Jesus called a little child unto him, and set him in the midst of them, ³ And said, Verily I say unto you, Except ye be converted, and become as little children, ye shall not enter into the kingdom of heaven. ⁴ Whosoever therefore shall humble himself as this little child, the same is greatest in the kingdom of heaven. ⁵ And whoso shall receive one such little child in my name receiveth me. ⁶ But whoso shall offend one of these little ones which believe in me, it were better for him that a millstone were hanged about his neck, and that he were drowned in the depth of the sea.

²¹ Then came Peter to him, and said, Lord, how oft shall my brother sin against me, and I forgive him? till seven times? ²² Jesus saith unto him, I say not unto thee, Until seven times: but, Until seventy times seven. ²³ Therefore is the kingdom of heaven likened unto a certain king, which would take account of his servants. ²⁴ And when he had begun to reckon, one was brought unto him, which owed him ten thousand talents. ²⁵ But forasmuch as he had not to pay, his lord commanded him to be sold, and his wife, and children, and all that he had, and payment to be made. ²⁶ The servant therefore fell down, and worshipped him, saying, Lord, have patience with me, and I will pay thee all. ²⁷ Then the lord of that servant was moved with compassion, and loosed him, and forgave him the debt. ²⁸ But the same servant went out,

and found one of his fellow servants, which owed him an hundred pence: and he laid hands on him, and took him by the throat, saying, Pay me that thou owest. [29] And his fellowservant fell down at his feet, and besought him, saying, Have patience with me, and I will pay thee all. [30] And he would not: but went and cast him into prison, till he should pay the debt. [31] So when his fellow servants saw what was done, they were very sorry, and came and told unto their lord all that was done. [32] Then his lord, after that he had called him, said unto him, O thou wicked servant, I forgave thee all that debt, because thou desiredst me: [33] Shouldest not thou also have had compassion on thy fellowservant, even as I had pity on thee? [34] And his lord was wroth, and delivered him to the tormentors, till he should pay all that was due unto him. [35] So likewise shall my heavenly Father do also unto you, if ye from your hearts forgive not every one his brother their trespasses.

It is important to look at some scriptures and see what the Bible says about an unforgiving spirit. We will then take our cue from these biblical admonitions. In Matthew 18:1-6 and 21-22, we will find a classical admonition, which if properly considered, can help us deal with resentment.

A child does not harbour evil in his heart; he easily forgives and carries on as if nothing wrong ever happened. Christ admonishes us to forgive seventy times seven times, which is tantamount to forgiving without recording wrongs done against you. Matthew 18 from verse 1 through 35, speaks of the danger of what can happen to those who refuse to deal with an unforgiving spirit in their lives. It says they will end up in outer darkness, where there is gnashing of the teeth, where the tormentors are.

Furthermore, when we look at Paul's admonition to Philemon, he was emphatic that Philemon should forgive Onesimus of all he did to him, to the extent of requesting that all that Onesimus had done or owed should be put in Paul's account. (See Philemon)

Matthew 6 (KJV)

> [9] After this manner therefore pray ye: Our Father which art in heaven, Hallowed be thy name. [10] Thy kingdom come, Thy will be done in earth, as it is in heaven. [11] Give us this day our daily bread. [12] And forgive us our debts, as we forgive our debtors. [13] And lead us not into temptation, but deliver us from evil: For thine is the kingdom, and the power, and the glory, for ever. Amen. [14] For if ye forgive men their trespasses, your heavenly Father will also forgive you: [15] But if ye forgive not men their trespasses, neither will your Father forgive your trespasses.

The Lord's Prayer is one scripture that is so strong and speaks highly of this issue of an unforgiving spirit and why we should not allow it to be resident in our hearts. In it, the Lord insisted that we should pray to God for forgiveness of our sins even as we forgive those who have offended us. As our Lord insisted, if we refuse to forgive those who have offended us, our Father in Heaven will also not forgive us our trespasses. The weight of this is one that should make us embrace a forgiving spirit.

156

DEALING WITH AN UNFORGIVING SPIRIT

Colossians 3 (KJV)

> [8] But now ye also put off all these; anger, wrath, malice, blasphemy, filthy communication out of your mouth. [9] Lie not one to another, seeing that ye have put off the old man with his deeds; [10] And have put on the new man, which is renewed in knowledge after the image of him that created him: [11] Where there is neither Greek nor Jew, circumcision nor uncircumcision, Barbarian, Scythian, bond nor free: but Christ is all, and in all. [12] Put on therefore, as the elect of God, holy and beloved, bowels of mercies, kindness, humbleness of mind, meekness, longsuffering; [13] Forbearing one another, and forgiving one another, if any man have a quarrel against any: even as Christ forgave you, so also do ye. [14] And above all these things put on charity, which is the bond of perfectness.

In Colossians 3:8-14, Paul admonishes us to put away evil things. In verse 13, he zeroed in on the issue of forgiveness when he said,

> 'Forbearing one another, and forgiving one another, if any man have a quarrel against any: even as Christ forgave you, so also do ye'.

We don't have an option. Christ has set the example and if you are His follower, you just have to follow in His footsteps else your followership of Christ will be suspect. If you are His, show it by your heart being full of forgiveness and devoid of an unforgiving spirit.

In 1st Peter 2:1-2, Peter admonished us to

> 'Lay aside all malice, and all guile, and hypocrisies, and envy, and all evil speaking, As new born babes, desire the sincere

milk of the Word, that ye may grow thereby'.

This admonishes us to lay aside the sources of an unforgiving spirit. He desires for us to be free from any agent that can whip up this evil spirit in us, he rather desires for us to be like new born babies who do not have the capacity to hold grudges.

We should not let the weight of an unforgiving spirit weigh us down; God has done so much for us. Even when we were neck deep in sin, He picked us up, cleansed us and forgave us. He has been our protector, guide and supplier. He has been kind to us. Although we kept sinning after He forgave and saved us, He has not killed us. His mercies and grace have remained our portion. When we cry to Him, He forgives. So why can't we let go of whatsoever that is holding us down and forgive? We are recipients of amazing forgiveness. Let us also imbibe that Christ-like Spirit.

This is the kind of spirit that overwhelmed Stephen in Acts of the Apostles 7:60, when he lifted up his voice and cried as he was being martyred,

'Lord, lay not this sin to their charge………'.

He followed in His Master's footsteps. Let's imbibe the words our Lord Jesus said as He was being crucified on the cross:

'Father forgive them, for they know not what they do'. (Luke

DEALING WITH AN UNFORGIVING SPIRIT

Chapter 23 verse 34).

Let us imbibe this spirit and mind. Christ's life – a life full of forgiveness - is one we should seek to model. Let us extend this wonderful spirit of forgiveness to all those who have wronged us knowingly or unknowingly.

CHAPTER 14

OUR SALVATION: WHAT A BEAUTIFUL THING

The Cleansing Power of the Blood of our Lord Jesus

In this chapter, we will look at the tedious route our Lord Jesus went through to bring us our beautiful salvation. Understanding and appreciating what the Lord did for us will surely help us imbibe the spirit of forgiveness.

In 1970, I was seventeen years old. It was just after the Nigerian Civil War and the Scripture Union, a wonderful Christian society that was all over the schools drawing students to the Lord, had massive Christian outreach in my town. I was invited to one of their meetings and the preacher spoke to us about the need for us to give our lives to Christ. He talked about the love of Christ and what Christ did for us; how He went to the cross, suffered and shed His Blood on our behalf; how all of this was for us to become children of God if we accept Him as our personal Saviour and Lord. After his speech, he made so much impression in quite a number of us and we answered the altar call. We came out en masse, prayed the sinner's prayer and gave our lives to Christ at that meeting. Since that day in 1970, I have never gone back but has kept the faith by God's grace.

I want us to look critically at what our Lord Jesus did for us. Let's consider the genesis of His action and by so doing see from His standpoint why we must live a life full of only forgiveness for those who offend us. What Christ did for us is far deeper than the content of the sinner's prayer. I want us to look at the genesis of what Christ did. Why did He do what He did? What did He intend to achieve? How does it affect us today as believers? For us to get the real kernel of it all, we have to go back to the beginning, to Leviticus chapter 16. This is the scripture that really encapsulates the completeness of the coming of the Lord and of everything that happened to the Lord Jesus from the time He was 30 years old to the time he was 33 and a half years old.

Leviticus 16 (KJV)

> [1] And the LORD spake unto Moses after the death of the two sons of Aaron, when they offered before the LORD, and died; [2] And the LORD said unto Moses, Speak unto Aaron thy brother, that he come not at all times into the holy place within the vail before the mercy seat, which is upon the ark; that he die not: for I will appear in the cloud upon the mercy seat. [3] Thus shall Aaron come into the holy place: with a young bullock for a sin offering, and a ram for a burnt offering. [4] He shall put on the holy linen coat, and he shall have the linen breeches upon his flesh, and shall be girded with a linen girdle, and with the linen mitre shall he be attired: these are holy garments; therefore shall he wash his flesh in water, and so put them on. [5] And he shall take of the congregation of the children of Israel two kids of the goats for a sin offering, and one ram for a burnt offering. [6] And Aaron shall offer his bullock of the sin offering, which is for himself, and make an atonement for himself, and for his house. [7] And he shall take the two goats, and present them before the LORD at the door of the tabernacle of the

congregation. [8] And Aaron shall cast lots upon the two goats; one lot for the LORD, and the other lot for the scapegoat. [9] And Aaron shall bring the goat upon which the LORD's lot fell, and offer him for a sin offering. [10] But the goat, on which the lot fell to be the scapegoat, shall be presented alive before the LORD, to make an atonement with him, and to let him go for a scapegoat into the wilderness. [11] And Aaron shall bring the bullock of the sin offering, which is for himself, and shall make an atonement for himself, and for his house, and shall kill the bullock of the sin offering which is for himself: [12] And he shall take a censer full of burning coals of fire from off the altar before the LORD, and his hands full of sweet incense beaten small, and bring it within the vail: [13] And he shall put the incense upon the fire before the LORD, that the cloud of the incense may cover the mercy seat that is upon the testimony, that he die not: [14] And he shall take of the blood of the bullock, and sprinkle it with his finger upon the mercy seat eastward; and before the mercy seat shall he sprinkle of the blood with his finger seven times. [15] Then shall he kill the goat of the sin offering, that is for the people, and bring his blood within the vail, and do with that blood as he did with the blood of the bullock, and sprinkle it upon the mercy seat, and before the mercy seat: [16] And he shall make an atonement for the holy place, because of the uncleanness of the children of Israel, and because of their transgressions in all their sins: and so shall he do for the tabernacle of the congregation, that remaineth among them in the midst of their uncleanness. [17] And there shall be no man in the tabernacle of the congregation when he goeth in to make an atonement in the holy place, until he come out, and have made an atonement for himself, and for his household, and for all the congregation of Israel. [18] And he shall go out unto the altar that is before the LORD, and make an atonement for it; and shall take of the blood of the bullock, and of the blood of the goat, and put it upon the horns of the altar round about. [19] And he shall sprinkle of the blood upon it with his finger seven times, and cleanse it, and hallow it from the uncleanness of the children of Israel. [20] And when he hath made an end of reconciling the holy place, and the tabernacle of the congregation, and the altar, he shall bring the live goat: [21] And Aaron shall lay both his hands upon the head of the live goat, and confess over him all the iniquities of the children of Israel, and all their transgressions in all their sins, putting them upon the head of the goat, and shall send him away by the hand of a fit man into the wilderness: [22] And the goat shall bear upon him all their iniquities unto a land not inhabited: and he shall let go the goat in the wilderness. [23] And Aaron shall come into the tabernacle of the congregation, and shall put off the linen garments, which he put on when he went into the holy place, and shall leave them there: [24] And he shall wash his flesh with water in the holy place, and put on his garments, and come forth, and offer his burnt offering, and the burnt offering of the people, and make an atonement for himself, and for the people. [25] And the fat of the sin offering shall he burn upon the altar. [26] And he that let go the goat for the scapegoat shall wash his clothes, and bathe his flesh in water, and afterward come into the camp. [27] And the bullock for the sin offering, and the goat for the sin offering, whose blood was brought in to make atonement in the holy place, shall one carry forth without the camp; and they shall burn in the fire their skins, and their flesh, and their dung. [28] And he that burneth them shall wash his clothes, and bathe his flesh in water, and afterward he shall come into the camp. [29] And this shall be a statute for ever unto you: that in the seventh month, on the tenth day of the month, ye shall afflict your souls, and do no work at all, whether it be one of your own country, or a stranger that sojourneth among you: [30] For on that day shall the priest make an atonement for you, to cleanse you, that ye may be clean from all your sins before the LORD. [31] It shall be a sabbath of rest unto you, and ye shall afflict your souls, by a statute for ever. [32] And the priest, whom he shall anoint, *and whom he shall consecrate to minister in the priest's office in his father's stead, shall make the atonement, and shall put on the linen clothes, even the holy garments: ³³ And he shall make an atonement for the holy sanctuary, and he shall make an atonement for the tabernacle of the congregation, and for the altar, and he shall make an atonement for the priests, and for all the people of the congregation. ³⁴ And this shall be an everlasting statute unto you, to make an atonement for the children of Israel for all their sins once a year. And he did as the LORD commanded Moses.*

In the above account, Leviticus records that when the Lord spoke to Aaron, He told him that on the Day of Atonement, you have to bring a bullock for yourself and your family and two goats for the children of Israel. The Day of Atonement in Hebrew is called the Yom Kippur. Yom Kippur is the holiest day in Israel. If we go back to Leviticus chapter 16, the Lord gave the Children of Israel a word concerning the Yom Kippur. From verse 29, He said this shall be a statue forever unto you, that in the seventh month and on the 10th day of the month, you shall afflict your souls, and do no work at all, whether it be one of your own country or by a stranger that sojourneth among you, for on that day shall the priest make an atonement for you to cleanse you that you may be clean from all your sins before the Lord. On Yom Kippur, everyone in Israel – free born and slaves, sojourners and strangers –no one is permitted to do any work. No one, not even a cattle is permitted to do any work. That day is separated unto the Lord. It is the day you afflict your soul and being. It is the day you remain before the Lord and an atonement is made for all your sins of the year.

In 1973, the Arabs ganged up and battled Israel on the Yom Kippur day because it is well known that Israel cannot go to battle that day as they do nothing except to remain in the presence of the Lord. But the Arabs made a mistake because that was a day that the Lord separated unto Himself. When the Arabs came, they nearly overran Israel but the Lord turned the battle at the gate because that was a day dedicated unto Him for the delivering of Israel from all their sins even if they are still practising it after the Lord Jesus fulfilled it.

You may wonder what this has to do with us today. Well, the two goats mentioned in the scripture above are very significant. Grasping the significance of these two goats and how they are related to what the Lord Jesus did for us is important. On Yom Kippur, the high priest will present the two goats before the tabernacle and the Lord. Lots will be cast for the two goats before the Lord. One goat will be slaughtered and its blood sprinkled before the altar and the Ark. The second goat would become a scapegoat and the high priest will lay his hands upon this goat and confess all the sins of the children of Israel for one full year. After this, the goat will be given to a fit man, one without blemish and who has a good standing before the Lord. The man will lead this goat –the scapegoat– into the wilderness. Symbolically, the goat becomes the scapegoat and carries all the sins of the Israelite into the wilderness.

The two goats – one as the scapegoat that will be led by a fit man into the wilderness, and the second goat, for slaughter so that its blood may be sprinkled before the Lord on behalf of every Israelite for the atonement performed by the high priest.

In Exodus 25:40, the Lord was clear in his instructions while speaking to Moses. He instructed Moses to ensure that everything that he does follows the pattern of what He has shown him on the mount. So, this was a figment and picture of what is going on in the Heavens. Being a shadow of things to come, if the Lord Jesus was to fulfil the law, then He must not only be the goat for sacrifice, He must also be the scapegoat. It is therefore important to know that Jesus fulfilled the role of the two goats. In Matthew 5:17, Lord Jesus said,

> 'think not that I have come to destroy the law or the prophets, I have not come to destroy but to fulfil'.

In John 19:28, the scripture said,

> '…and after this, Jesus knowing that things were now accomplished that the scripture might be fulfilled he said, "I thirst'.

At this juncture, He knew that everything has been taken care of. In John 19:30 reads,

> 'when Jesus therefore received the vinegar, He said it is finished and bowed His Head and gave up the ghost'.

OUR SALVATION: WHAT A BEAUTIFUL THING

This showed that He has accomplished the purpose for which he came. To accomplish this propose in totality, He had to take on the roles of both goats. He needed to fulfil the role of the two goats in order for our salvation to be complete. Praise the Lord.

Let's see how He did this. In **John 1:29 - 36**, the scripture said

> [29] The next day John seeth Jesus coming unto him, and saith, Behold the Lamb of God, which taketh away the sin of the world. [30] This is he of whom I said, After me cometh a man which is preferred before me: for he was before me. [31] And I knew him not: but that he should be made manifest to Israel, therefore am I come baptizing with water. [32] And John bare record, saying, I saw the Spirit descending from heaven like a dove, and it abode upon him. [33] And I knew him not: but he that sent me to baptize with water, the same said unto me, Upon whom thou shalt see the Spirit descending, and remaining on him, the same is he which baptizeth with the Holy Ghost. [34] And I saw, and bare record that this is the Son of God. [35] Again the next day after John stood, and two of his disciples; [36] And looking upon Jesus as he walked, he saith, Behold the Lamb of God!

This explains why John the Baptist exclaimed upon seeing Jesus coming unto him, 'behold the Lamb of God who takes away the sins of the world'. In verse 32, John the Baptist said,

> 'I saw the Spirit of God descending like a Dove upon Him and I knew Him not'.

John explained that though he baptized Jesus with water, the One who sent him has informed him that whosoever the Spirit will descend upon will be baptised with the Holy Spirit. The Holy Spirit did two great things at the baptism: the first, His announcement to the world and the second, we will see in Matthew 3:11-17 and 4:1;

Matthew 3:11 - 17 (KJV)

[11] I indeed baptize you with water unto repentance. but he that cometh after me is mightier than I, whose shoes I am not worthy to bear: he shall baptize you with the Holy Ghost, and with fire: [12] Whose fan is in his hand, and he will throughly purge his floor, and gather his wheat into the garner; but he will burn up the chaff with unquenchable fire. [13] Then cometh Jesus from Galilee to Jordan unto John, to be baptized of him. [14] But John forbad him, saying, I have need to be baptized of thee, and comest thou to me? [15] And Jesus answering said unto him, Suffer it to be so now: for thus it becometh us to fulfil all righteousness. Then he suffered him. [16] And Jesus, when he was baptized, went up straightway out of the water: and, lo, the heavens were opened unto him, and he saw the Spirit of God descending like a dove, and lighting upon him: [17] And lo a voice from heaven, saying, This is my beloved Son, in whom I am well pleased.

Matthew Chapter 4:1 - 11 (KJV)

[1] Then was Jesus led up of the Spirit into the wilderness to be tempted of the devil. [2] And when he had fasted forty days and forty nights, he was afterward an hungred. [3] And when the tempter came to him, he said, If thou be the Son of God, command that these stones be made bread. [4] But he answered and said, It is written, Man shall not live by bread alone, but by every word that proceedeth out of the mouth of God. [5] Then the devil taketh him up into the holy city, and

setteth him on a pinnacle of the temple, [6] And saith unto him, If thou be the Son of God, cast thyself down: for it is written, He shall give his angels charge concerning thee: and in their hands they shall bear thee up, lest at any time thou dash thy foot against a stone. [7] Jesus said unto him, It is written again, Thou shalt not tempt the Lord thy God. [8] Again, the devil taketh him up into an exceeding high mountain, and sheweth him all the kingdoms of the world, and the glory of them; [9] And saith unto him, All these things will I give thee, if thou wilt fall down and worship me. [10] Then saith Jesus unto him, Get thee hence, Satan: for it is written, Thou shalt worship the Lord thy God, and him only shalt thou serve. [11] Then the devil leaveth him, and, behold, angels came and ministered unto him.

From Matthew's account, Jesus went from Galilee to Jordan to meet John for His baptism. This baptism is very significant because you see when you baptize, you lay hands. It is also proper to know who John the Baptist is. If we go back to Luke chapter 1, we would see the root of John the Baptist. His father, Zechariah was of the line of Abia, a priestly lineage, and his mother Elizabeth was traced right down to Aaron the first High Priest of Israel. So we can see that both Zachariah and his wife were of the priestly order. Zachariah was the priest in charge of the temple at the time that John was born. John having come from the lineage of Aaron was a priest also. John's birth and lineage is symbolic because only a priest can lay hands on the scapegoat and condemn the goat that will be sacrificed and the blood sprinkled before the Lord.

Jesus came to fulfil the law, so every aspect of the law has to be fulfilled for our salvation to be complete. If every aspect is fulfilled, we will have a beautiful salvation. John refused to baptise Jesus because he saw a higher authority and was willing to submit to it. Bless the Name of the Lord. Amen. Jesus' reply to John was symbolic, too: 'unto him suffer it to be so now'. With this, Christ acknowledged that it was just temporarily as all righteousness concerning the law would be fulfilled. John obliged Him and Jesus after His baptism came out of the water and the heavens were opened unto Him. Jesus saw the Spirit of God descending like a Dove upon Him and heard a voice from heaven saying and acknowledging that He was God's Beloved Son in whom He is well pleased.

After the Spirit descended upon Christ, a dramatic event occurred: the Holy Spirit led Him into the wilderness to be tempted by the devil. This was the second great event of the Holy Spirit at Christ's baptism.

As recorded in the account in Leviticus 16, when the Priest has laid his hands on the scapegoat and confessed the sins of the people of Israel, a FIT man approved of God, leads the scapegoat into the wilderness.

John of the priestly order confessed that Jesus was the Lamb of God who takes away the sins of the world and laid hands on Him as the Scapegoat afterwards. By so doing, John transferred upon Him all the sins of the whole world and baptized Him in the Jordan. And immediately Jesus came out of the water, The FIT Man – the Holy Spirit, the man without blemish – led Him into the wilderness as the Scapegoat for our redemption. Praise the Lord. Amen.

If John had not laid hands on Jesus and transferred the whole sins of the world onto Him, His death on the cross will not have benefited us because every aspect of this scripture must be fulfilled for our salvation to be complete. Every aspect of the shadow that was represented by the two goats must be fulfilled in JESUS. That was why the Lord Jesus insisted that John must baptize Him so that all aspect of the Law of Atonement would be fulfilled in Him.

When Christ became the scapegoat, the second part of the Atonement had to be accomplished. Although the sins of the world had now been laid on the Lamb, He had to pay the punishment for the sins laid on Him. He who knew no sin became sin so that we could be set free from our sins. Jesus carried the sin of the world –past, present and future– on His shoulders when John laid hands on Him. But because God must punish sin, Jesus needed to pay the penalty for the sins by going to the cross. If the sins were not laid on Jesus and He went to the cross, it would have been injustice to crucify an innocent man.

Although Jesus wept and pleaded for God to let this cup pass over Him, God refused because He now bore the sins of the world and must face judgement on the cross. In essence, God was saying: 'You must go to the cross, my son. Sin must be judged and you have become an embodiment of the sins of the world, so you must be judged and punished. John laid hands on you and transferred the sins of the world to you. The Holy Spirit led you into the wilderness as the Scapegoat, so there is no escape for you. You must be judged and punished because every sin must be judged and punished'.

John Chapter 18: 12 – 14 (KJV)

> [12] Then the band and the captain and officers of the Jews took Jesus, and bound him, [13] And led him away to Annas first; for he was father in law to Caiaphas, which was the high priest that same year. [14] Now Caiaphas was he, which gave counsel to the Jews, that it was expedient that one man should die for the people.

In verse 14, the high priest, Caiaphas said, 'that it was expedient that one man should die for the people'. The high priest believed that it was expedient that this Man who became sin for the whole world should die because it is pragmatic for one Man to die for all. Caiaphas at this time was prophesying.

Many of us have not understood our salvation from this aspect but this is actually very important. Jesus needed to pay the price and go to Golgotha to pay for the sins that were laid on Him.

John 19 (KJV)

> 1 Then Pilate therefore took Jesus, and scourged him. [2] And the soldiers platted a crown of thorns, and put it on his head, and they put on him a purple robe, [3] And said, Hail, King of the Jews! and they smote him with their hands. [4] Pilate therefore went forth again, and saith unto them,

OUR SALVATION: WHAT A BEAUTIFUL THING

*Behold, I bring him forth to you, that ye may know that I find no fault in him. [5] Then came Jesus forth, wearing the crown of thorns, and the purple robe. And Pilate saith unto them, Behold the man! [6] When the chief priests therefore and officers saw him, they cried out, saying, Crucify him, crucify him. Pilate saith unto them, Take ye him, and crucify him: for I find no fault in him. [7] The Jews answered him, We have a law, and by our law he ought to die, because he made himself the Son of God. [8] When Pilate therefore heard that saying, he was the more afraid; [9] And went again into the judgment hall, and saith unto Jesus, Whence art thou? But Jesus gave him no answer. [10] Then saith Pilate unto him, Speakest thou not unto me? knowest thou not that I have power to crucify thee, and have power to release thee? [11] Jesus answered, Thou couldest have no power at all against me, except it were given thee from above: therefore he that delivered me unto thee hath the greater sin. [12] And from thenceforth Pilate sought to release him: but the Jews cried out, saying, If thou let this man go, thou art not Caesar's friend: whosoever maketh himself a king speaketh against Caesar. [13] When Pilate therefore heard that saying, he brought Jesus forth, and sat down in the judgment seat in a place that is called the Pavement, but in the Hebrew, Gabbatha. [14] And it was the preparation of the passover, and about the sixth hour: and he saith unto the Jews, Behold your King! [15] But they cried out, Away with him, away with him, crucify him. Pilate saith unto them, Shall I crucify your King? The chief priests answered, We have no king but Caesar. [16] Then delivered he him therefore unto them to be crucified. And they took Jesus, and led him away. [17] And he bearing his cross went forth into a place called the place of a skull, which is called in the Hebrew Golgotha: [18] Where they crucified him, and two other with him, on either side one, and Jesus in the midst. [19] And Pilate wrote a title, and put it on the cross. And the writing was JESUS OF **NAZARETH THE KING OF THE JEWS**. [20] This title then read many of the Jews: for the* place where Jesus was crucified was nigh to the city: and it was written in Hebrew, and Greek, and Latin. ²¹ Then said the chief priests of the Jews to Pilate, Write not, The King of the Jews; but that he said, I am King of the Jews. ²² Pilate answered, What I have written I have written. ²³ Then the soldiers, when they had crucified Jesus, took his garments, and made four parts, to every soldier a part; and also his coat: now the coat was without seam, woven from the top throughout. ²⁴ They said therefore among themselves, Let us not rend it, but cast lots for it, whose it shall be: that the scripture might be fulfilled, which saith, They parted my raiment among them, and for my vesture they did cast lots. These things therefore the soldiers did. ²⁵ Now there stood by the cross of Jesus his mother, and his mother's sister, Mary the wife of Cleophas, and Mary Magdalene. ²⁶ When Jesus therefore saw his mother, and the disciple standing by, whom he loved, he saith unto his mother, Woman, behold thy son! ²⁷ Then saith he to the disciple, Behold thy mother! And from that hour that disciple took her unto his own home. ²⁸ After this, Jesus knowing that all things were now accomplished, that the scripture might be fulfilled, saith, I thirst. ²⁹ Now there was set a vessel full of vinegar: and they filled a spunge with vinegar, and put it upon hyssop, and put it to his mouth. ³⁰ When Jesus therefore had received the vinegar, he said, It is finished: and he bowed his head, and gave up the ghost. ³¹ The Jews therefore, because it was the preparation, that the bodies should not remain upon the cross on the sabbath day, (for that sabbath day was an high day,) besought Pilate that their legs might be broken, and that they might be taken away. ³² Then came the soldiers, and brake the legs of the first, and of the other which was crucified with him. ³³ But when they came to Jesus, and saw that he was dead already, they brake not his legs: ³⁴ But one of the soldiers with a spear pierced his side, and forthwith came there out blood and water. ³⁵ And he that saw it bare record, and his record is true: and he knoweth that he saith true, that ye might believe. ³⁶ For these things were done, that the scripture should be fulfilled, A bone of him shall not be broken. ³⁷ And again another scripture saith, They shall look on him whom they pierced. ³⁸ And after this Joseph of Arimathaea, being a disciple of Jesus, but secretly for fear of the Jews, besought Pilate that he might take away the body of Jesus: and Pilate gave him leave. He came therefore, and took the body of Jesus. ³⁹ And there came also Nicodemus, which at the first came to Jesus by night, and brought a mixture of myrrh and aloes, about an hundred pound weight. ⁴⁰ Then took they the body of Jesus, and wound it in linen clothes with the spices, as the manner of the Jews is to bury. ⁴¹ Now in the place where he was crucified there was a garden; and in the garden a new sepulchre, wherein was never man yet laid. ⁴² There laid they Jesus therefore because of the Jews' preparation day; for the sepulchre was nigh at hand.

In John 19, we see the second goat that was offered. And as Jesus was hung on the Cross, the Bible asserted that when He saw He had fulfilled all that was demanded by the Law – the full payment for our sins – He cried that it was finished. God exerted His full revenge for our sins on Him at the cross. In Chapter 19, we see the true picture of the second goat being fulfilled, Jesus received the full punishment for our sins upon Himself and was crucified for that. When he came to the point where He realised that everything has been accomplished, the scapegoat and the sacrificial goat they have both been accomplished in Him, then He said I thirst. Once that hyssop mingled with vinegar was given to Him, He exclaimed with power and with authority, it is finished.

Dear Friends, your sins are finished as a result of the finished work of Christ our Lord. Our enemy, the devil has no right to hold you in bondage again with respect to your sins. Lord Jesus took it all on Himself and declared you free, unless of course, you have not given your life to Him. John 1:12 said that

'for as many as received Him, to them He gave power to become the sons of God'.

Therefore if you have become a son as a result of receiving Him into your life, there is no more condemnation to you who is called according to the calling of the Lord. That's what the Bible says.

Dear Friends, we need to sit back again and reconsider our salvation and appreciate what the Lord Jesus did for us continuously. He became the scapegoat and the sacrificial goat that we may be called His own. Hallelujah! Even better, He did not stop there – He resurrected. An account of Jesus' resurrection is found in John 20.

John 20 (KJV)

1 *The first day of the week cometh Mary Magdalene early, when it was yet dark, unto the sepulchre, and seeth the stone taken away from the sepulchre.* [2] *Then she runneth, and cometh to Simon Peter, and to the other disciple, whom Jesus loved, and saith unto them, They have taken away the* LORD *out of the sepulchre, and we know not where they have laid him.* [3] *Peter therefore went forth, and that other disciple, and came to the sepulchre.* [4] *So they ran both together: and the other disciple did outrun Peter, and came*

first to the sepulchre. [5] And he stooping down, and looking in, saw the linen clothes lying; yet went he not in. [6] Then cometh Simon Peter following him, and went into the sepulchre, and seeth the linen clothes lie, [7] And the napkin, that was about his head, not lying with the linen clothes, but wrapped together in a place by itself. [8] Then went in also that other disciple, which came first to the sepulchre, and he saw, and believed. [9] For as yet they knew not the scripture, that he must rise again from the dead. [10] Then the disciples went away again unto their own home. [11] But Mary stood without at the sepulchre weeping: and as she wept, she stooped down, and looked into the sepulchre, [12] And seeth two angels in white sitting, the one at the head, and the other at the feet, where the body of Jesus had lain. [13] And they say unto her, Woman, why weepest thou? She saith unto them, Because they have taken away my LORD, and I know not where they have laid him. [14] And when she had thus said, she turned herself back, and saw Jesus standing, and knew not that it was Jesus. [15] Jesus saith unto her, Woman, why weepest thou? whom seekest thou? She, supposing him to be the gardener, saith unto him, Sir, if thou have borne him hence, tell me where thou hast laid him, and I will take him away. [16] Jesus saith unto her, Mary. She turned herself, and saith unto him, Rabboni; which is to say, Master. [17] Jesus saith unto her, Touch me not; for I am not yet ascended to my Father: but go to my brethren, and say unto them, I ascend unto my Father, and your Father; and to my God, and your God. [18] Mary Magdalene came and told the disciples that she had seen the LORD, and that he had spoken these things unto her. [19] Then the same day at evening, being the first day of the week, when the doors were shut where the disciples were assembled for fear of the Jews, came Jesus and stood in the midst, and saith unto them, Peace be unto you. [20] And when he had so said, he shewed unto them his hands and his side. Then were the disciples glad, when they saw the LORD. [21] Then said Jesus to them again, Peace be *unto you: as my Father hath sent me, even so send I you.* [22] *And when he had said this, he breathed on them, and saith unto them, Receive ye the Holy Ghost:* [23] *Whose soever sins ye remit, they are remitted unto them; and whose soever sins ye retain, they are retained.* [24] *But Thomas, one of the twelve, called Didymus, was not with them when Jesus came.* [25] *The other disciples therefore said unto him, We have seen the LORD. But he said unto them, Except I shall see in his hands the print of the nails, and put my finger into the print of the nails, and thrust my hand into his side, I will not believe.* [26] *And after eight days again his disciples were within, and Thomas with them: then came Jesus, the doors being shut, and stood in the midst, and said, Peace be unto you.* [27] *Then saith he to Thomas, Reach hither thy finger, and behold my hands; and reach hither thy hand, and thrust it into my side: and be not faithless, but believing.* [28] *And Thomas answered and said unto him, My LORD and my God.* [29] *Jesus saith unto him, Thomas, because thou hast seen me, thou hast believed: blessed are they that have not seen, and yet have believed.* [30] *And many other signs truly did Jesus in the presence of his disciples, which are not written in this book:* [31] *But these are written, that ye might believe that Jesus is the Christ, the Son of God; and that believing ye might have life through his name.*

John 21 (KJV)

[1] *After these things Jesus shewed himself again to the disciples at the sea of Tiberias; and on this wise shewed he himself.* [2] *There were together Simon Peter, and Thomas called Didymus, and Nathanael of Cana in Galilee, and the sons of Zebedee, and two other of his disciples.* [3] *Simon Peter saith unto them, I go a fishing. They say unto him, We also go with thee. They went forth, and entered into a ship immediately; and that night they caught nothing.* [4] *But when*

the morning was now come, Jesus stood on the shore: but the disciples knew not that it was Jesus. [5] Then Jesus saith unto them, Children, have ye any meat? They answered him, No. [6] And he said unto them, Cast the net on the right side of the ship, and ye shall find. They cast therefore, and now they were not able to draw it for the multitude of fishes. [7] Therefore that disciple whom Jesus loved saith unto Peter, It is the Lord. Now when Simon Peter heard that it was the Lord, he girt his fisher's coat unto him, (for he was naked,) and did cast himself into the sea. [8] And the other disciples came in a little ship; (for they were not far from land, but as it were two hundred cubits,) dragging the net with fishes. [9] As soon then as they were come to land, they saw a fire of coals there, and fish laid thereon, and bread. [10] Jesus saith unto them, Bring of the fish which ye have now caught. [11] Simon Peter went up, and drew the net to land full of great fishes, an hundred and fifty and three: and for all there were so many, yet was not the net broken. [12] Jesus saith unto them, Come and dine. And none of the disciples durst ask him, Who art thou? knowing that it was the Lord. [13] Jesus then cometh, and taketh bread, and giveth them, and fish likewise. [14] This is now the third time that Jesus shewed himself to his disciples, after that he was risen from the dead. [15] So when they had dined, Jesus saith to Simon Peter, Simon, son of Jonas, lovest thou me more than these? He saith unto him, Yea, Lord; thou knowest that I love thee. He saith unto him, Feed my lambs. [16] He saith to him again the second time, Simon, son of Jonas, lovest thou me? He saith unto him, Yea, Lord; thou knowest that I love thee. He saith unto him, Feed my sheep. [17] He saith unto him the third time, Simon, son of Jonas, lovest thou me? Peter was grieved because he said unto him the third time, Lovest thou me? And he said unto him, Lord, thou knowest all things; thou knowest that I love thee. Jesus saith unto him, Feed my sheep. [18] Verily, verily, I say unto thee, When thou wast young, thou girdest thyself, and walkedst whither thou wouldest: but when thou shalt be old, thou shalt stretch forth thy hands, and another shall gird thee, and carry thee whither thou wouldest not. [19] This spake he, signifying by what death he should glorify God. And when he had spoken this, he saith unto him, Follow me. [20] Then Peter, turning about, seeth the disciple whom Jesus loved following; which also leaned on his breast at supper, and said, Lord, which is he that betrayeth thee? [21] Peter seeing him saith to Jesus, Lord, and what shall this man do? [22] Jesus saith unto him, If I will that he tarry till I come, what is that to thee? follow thou me. [23] Then went this saying abroad among the brethren, that that disciple should not die: yet Jesus said not unto him, He shall not die; but, If I will that he tarry till I come, what is that to thee? [24] This is the disciple which testifieth of these things, and wrote these things: and we know that his testimony is true. [25] And there are also many other things which Jesus did, the which, if they should be written every one, I suppose that even the world itself could not contain the books that should be written. Amen.

Acts 1 (KJV)

[1] The former treatise have I made, O Theophilus, of all that Jesus began both to do and teach, [2] Until the day in which he was taken up, after that he through the Holy Ghost had given commandments unto the apostles whom he had chosen: [3] To whom also he shewed himself alive after his passion by many infallible proofs, being seen of them forty days, and speaking of the things pertaining to the kingdom of God: [4] And, being assembled together with them, commanded them that they should not depart from Jerusalem, but wait for the promise of the Father, which, saith he, ye have heard of me. [5] For John truly baptized with water; but ye shall be baptized with the Holy Ghost not many days hence. [6] When they therefore were come together, they

asked of him, saying, Lord, wilt thou at this time restore again the kingdom to Israel? [7] And he said unto them, It is not for you to know the times or the seasons, which the Father hath put in his own power. [8] But ye shall receive power, after that the Holy Ghost is come upon you: and ye shall be witnesses unto me both in Jerusalem, and in all Judaea, and in Samaria, and unto the uttermost part of the earth. [9] And when he had spoken these things, while they beheld, he was taken up; and a cloud received him out of their sight. [10] And while they looked stedfastly toward heaven as he went up, behold, two men stood by them in white apparel; [11] Which also said, Ye men of Galilee, why stand ye gazing up into heaven? this same Jesus, which is taken up from you into heaven, shall so come in like manner as ye have seen him go into heaven. [12] Then returned they unto Jerusalem from the mount called Olivet, which is from Jerusalem a sabbath day's journey.

In John 20 and 21, we can read about His resurrection. Verses 1 to 14 of John 21 gave a vivid account of Jesus' life before His ascension. Acts 1: 4-11 gives an account of Jesus' ascension. These two events are significant because Christ not only resurrected but ascended. Glory be to God. Jesus ascended to set the captive free. He also went to the Heavens – a key event in His ascension. Aaron's actions were a shadow of things to come. Christ went to Heaven and sprinkled His blood on the Throne of God so that we will no longer be subjected to annual animal sacrifices. He did that once and it stands forever. God was saying, 'I have no taste for goats and bulls anymore. They do not satisfy me anymore'.

Hebrews 10 (KJV)

10 For the law having a shadow of good things to come, and not the very image of the things, can never with those sacrifices which they offered year by year continually make the comers thereunto perfect. 2 For then would they not have ceased to be offered? because that the worshippers once purged should have had no more conscience of sins. 3 But in those sacrifices there is a remembrance again made of sins every year. 4 For it is not possible that the blood of bulls and of goats should take away sins. 5 Wherefore when he cometh into the world, he saith, Sacrifice and offering thou wouldest not, but a body hast thou prepared me: 6 In burnt offerings and sacrifices for sin thou hast had no pleasure. 7 Then said I, Lo, I come (in the volume of the book it is written of me,) to do thy will, O God. 8 Above when he said, Sacrifice and offering and burnt offerings and offering for sin thou wouldest not, neither hadst pleasure therein; which are offered by the law; 9 Then said he, Lo, I come to do thy will, O God. He taketh away the first, that he may establish the second. 10 By the which will we are sanctified through the offering of the body of Jesus Christ once for all. 11 And every priest standeth daily ministering and offering oftentimes the same sacrifices, which can never take away sins: 12 But this man, after he had offered one sacrifice for sins for ever, sat down on the right hand of God; 13 From henceforth expecting till his enemies be made his footstool. 14 For by one offering he hath perfected for ever them that are sanctified. 15 Whereof the Holy Ghost also is a witness to us: for after that he had said before, 16 This is the covenant that I will make with them after those days, saith the Lord, I will put my laws into their hearts, and in their minds will I write them; 17 And their sins and iniquities will I remember no more. 18 Now where remission of these is, there is no more offering for sin.

Let Us Draw Near and Hold Fast

OUR SALVATION: WHAT A BEAUTIFUL THING

19 *Having therefore, brethren, boldness to enter into the holiest by the blood of Jesus,* 20 *By a new and living way, which he hath consecrated for us, through the veil, that is to say, his flesh;* 21 *And having an high priest over the house of God;* 22 *Let us draw near with a true heart in full assurance of faith, having our hearts sprinkled from an evil conscience, and our bodies washed with pure water.* 23 *Let us hold fast the profession of our faith without wavering; (for he is faithful that promised;)* 24 *And let us consider one another to provoke unto love and to good works:* 25 *Not forsaking the assembling of ourselves together, as the manner of some is; but exhorting one another: and so much the more, as ye see the day approaching.* 26 *For if we sin wilfully after that we have received the knowledge of the truth, there remaineth no more sacrifice for sins,* 27 *But a certain fearful looking for of judgment and fiery indignation, which shall devour the adversaries.* 28 *He that despised Moses' law died without mercy under two or three witnesses:* 29 *Of how much sorer punishment, suppose ye, shall he be thought worthy, who hath trodden under foot the Son of God, and hath counted the blood of the covenant, wherewith he was sanctified, an unholy thing, and hath done despite unto the Spirit of grace?* 30 *For we know him that hath said, Vengeance belongeth unto me, I will recompense, saith the Lord. And again, The Lord shall judge his people.* 31 *It is a fearful thing to fall into the hands of the living God.* 32 *But call to remembrance the former days, in which, after ye were illuminated, ye endured a great fight of afflictions;* 33 *Partly, whilst ye were made a gazingstock both by reproaches and afflictions; and partly, whilst ye became companions of them that were so used.* 34 *For ye had compassion of me in my bonds, and took joyfully the spoiling of your goods, knowing in yourselves that ye have in heaven a better and an enduring substance.* 35 *Cast not away therefore your confidence, which hath great recompence of reward.* 36 *For ye have need of patience, that, after ye have done the will of*

God, ye might receive the promise. 37 For yet a little while, and he that shall come will come, and will not tarry. 38 Now the just shall live by faith: but if any man draw back, my soul shall have no pleasure in him. 39 But we are not of them who draw back unto perdition; but of them that believe to the saving of the soul.

Hebrews 10 succinctly portrays the dilemma God was in as a result of the failed Aaronic atonement. The Lord Jesus had to offer Himself as the acceptable sacrifice that meets all of God's demands. He paid with His blood and life – an acceptable, sweet and beautiful sacrifice. Dear friends in the Lord, your salvation is complete.

1st Peter Chapter 1: 18 -25 (KJV)

[18] *Forasmuch as ye know that ye were not redeemed with corruptible things, as silver and gold, from your vain conversation received by tradition from your fathers;* [19] *But with the precious blood of Christ, as of a lamb without blemish and without spot:* [20] *Who verily was foreordained before the foundation of the world, but was manifest in these last times for you,* [21] *Who by him do believe in God, that raised him up from the dead, and gave him glory; that your faith and hope might be in God.* [22] *Seeing ye have purified your souls in obeying the truth through the Spirit unto unfeigned love of the brethren, see that ye love one another with a pure heart fervently:* [23] *Being born again, not of corruptible seed, but of incorruptible, by the word of God, which liveth and abideth for ever.* [24] *For all flesh is as grass, and all the glory of man as the flower of grass. The grass withereth, and the flower thereof falleth away:* [25] *But the word of the Lord endureth for ever. And this is the word which by the gospel is preached unto you.*

OUR SALVATION: WHAT A BEAUTIFUL THING

In 1st Peter 1:18-19, the Bible made it plain that Jesus was foreordained to be the acceptable Lamb without blemish for sacrifice. Verse 20 was emphatic in asking us who are partakers and beneficiaries of such a wonderful gift of forgiveness to have nothing but perfect love for one another. If you have this perfect love originating from your appreciation of what Christ did for you, you will not only radiate but overflow in a life of forgiveness.

> 'But with the precious blood of Christ as a Lamb without blemish and without spot, for as much as you know that you were not redeemed with corruptible things as silver and gold from your vain conversation received by tradition from your fathers that's with the precious blood of Christ as of a lamb without blemish and without spot was foreordained before the foundation of the world but was manifest in this last times for you, who by Him do believe in God that raised Him from the dead, and gave Him glory; that your faith and hope might be in God'.

It is a complete salvation – the salvation of everything that pertains to you. It is not a half measure salvation. That's why in Romans 8:32, Paul was emphatic in asking, what God could not give us if He could let His son die for us. Our salvation is so complete that the same power in our salvation is inherent in us. It enables us with the power to forgive those who sinned against us.

The Bible tells us about how our salvation encompasses both light and heavy afflictions and takes care of them all. This is why Jesus reaffirmed that all is finished. And indeed, nothing is left out. Glory be to God. Amen.

In 1st Peter 2:24-25, the Scripture says

> [24] Who his own self bare our sins in his own body on the tree, that we, being dead to sins, should live unto righteousness: by whose stripes ye were healed. [25] For ye were as sheep going astray; but are now returned unto the Shepherd and Bishop of your souls.

Our health, righteousness and prosperity is in this salvation. No aspects of the Day of Atonement was left out in Christ. Yom Kippur is a holy day but for believers in Christ, every day is our Yom Kippur. Yom Kippur speaks about one day and all that happened one year before the day. However, it is dead and expires after that day; everyone carries on again and waits for the next year's Yom Kippur. But the Blood of Jesus speaks forever – it is speaking even now as you are reading this book. Our Yom Kippur is forever and speaks on our behalf at all times.

Hebrews Chapter 10 verses 19 to 24

> [19] Having therefore, brethren, boldness to enter into the holiest by the blood of Jesus, [20] By a new and living way, which he hath consecrated for us, through the veil, that is to say, his flesh; [21] And having an high priest over the house of God; [22] Let us draw near with a true heart in full assurance of faith, having our hearts sprinkled from an evil conscience, and our bodies washed with pure water.

We have boldness to enter into the holiest place because of what Christ has done for us. The effects of what He did is not for one year or ten years – it is forever. Amen. Yom Kippur is done and people wait for the same time next year before they can do it again. But from the scripture above, we have the boldness to enter, not just the holy place, but the holiest place, the Throne of God because the Blood of the Final Yom Kippur, the Blood of Jesus speaks better things on our behalf. It always speaks forgiveness on our behalf.

The blood of Jesus makes us bold. His blood does not expire. It speaks now and will speak for me until the day He calls me home. The blood will continue to speak even while I am in Glory. Hallelujah. Amen.

So why should you not give your life to Christ, who became your scapegoat and sacrificial goat so He could give you an everlasting, ever speaking blood – a blood that can give you life at all times? Why will you not give your life to Him? Why will you not have faith and hope in this work that He has done? Dear friends, if you have given your life to Christ, your faith is without question. You have unrestricted access to the holiest place and all the resources you need to forgive any wrong done to you. You have all this because of what Jesus has done for you and the door He has opened for you. Christ has not only shown us the way, He has also provided us a way to deal with any unforgiving spirit.

I want us to see one Scripture **Luke Chapter 23 verses 13 to 26 (KJV)**

[13] And Pilate, when he had called together the chief priests and the rulers and the people, [14] Said unto them, Ye have brought this man unto me, as one that perverteth the people: and, behold, I, having examined him before you, have found no fault in this man touching those things whereof ye accuse him: [15] No, nor yet Herod: for I sent you to him; and, lo, nothing worthy of death is done unto him. [16] I will therefore chastise him, and release him. [17] (For of necessity he must release one unto them at the feast.) [18] And they cried out all at once, saying, Away with this man, and release unto us Barabbas: [19] (Who for a certain sedition made in the city, and for murder, was cast into prison.) [20] Pilate therefore, willing to release Jesus, spake again to them. [21] But they cried, saying, Crucify him, crucify him. [22] And he said unto them the third time, Why, what evil hath he done? I have found no cause of death in him: I will therefore chastise him, and let him go. [23] And they were instant with loud voices, requiring that he might be crucified. And the voices of them and of the chief priests prevailed. [24] And Pilate gave sentence that it should be as they required. [25] And he released unto them him that for sedition and murder was cast into prison, whom they had desired; but he delivered Jesus to their will. [26] And as they led him away, they laid hold upon one Simon, a Cyrenian, coming out of the country, and on him they laid the cross, that he might bear it after Jesus.

After thorough examination, Pilate found no fault in Jesus. Though the rants of the people were so great against Jesus, their accusations were baseless. Pilate was emphatic that even Herod found nothing worthy of death against Jesus. But yet He needed to die. As Pilate insisted on releasing Jesus, the crowd cried louder and rather preferred that Barabbas, a man who was thrown into prison for sedition and murder, be released unto them.

OUR SALVATION: WHAT A BEAUTIFUL THING

Pilate who did not know the ordinance and programme of God may have been even the enemy who was ready to abort the salvation of you and me. Jesus gave Barabbas His life just like He has given you your life and me, mine. Barabbas was set free but Jesus died having collected all our sins. He was like a refuse collector. All our filthy sins were laid on Him.

Dear Friends, I don't know if Barabbas ever appreciated what Christ did for him. Unfortunately, many of us today are not appreciative of what the Lord has done for us. We are so busy with ourselves and full of ourselves that we do not give a thought to what the Lord passed through to bring us to where we are today. You can conveniently hold someone in bondage and let hurts fester in your heart because you are not yet appreciative of Christ's work of salvation. All you are concerned about is revenge because you care about you alone. You don't give a hoot about the sufferings Christ passed through to bear your sins and gain God's forgiveness for you. If you remember this unmerited favour from God, nothing anyone does against you will be too much for your forgiveness.

I want to challenge you, dear friend to firstly consider your relationship with Christ. Are you born again? Have you really given your life to Christ? Have you sat back and considered all that Jesus did for you? Have you in all sincerity said, 'Lord Jesus, I appreciate what you did for me. Please come into my life and be my Lord and Saviour. Take away every sin that is in me and make me Your own. Turn me around to love You and to serve You and live my life ever appreciating what You did for me'?

If you have given your life to Jesus, why not sit back and appreciate what the Lord did for you. Are you so busy with yourself? Are you so full of your own life that you've forgotten this great gift God gave to you?

The Lord gave His best for you in order to obtain God's forgiveness for you. You deserved eternal death in the lake of fire but the Lord sacrificed Himself to rescue you from that eternal damnation. Let the Spirit of Jesus saturate and give you the enabling power to forgive all offenses. Amen.

CHAPTER 15

WHY SHOULD WE FORGIVE?

When we forgive, we do ourselves a great favour. Withholding forgiveness releases the bile of bitterness which can truncate our health situation. It can cause us trauma and high blood pressure. It can lead to all manners of diseases. We may get so carried away by plotting revenge that we end up blocking out other pressing and needful aspects of our living.

Spiritually, this will block the flow of communication between God and us. At this point, we will become separated from God and all our spirituality would become superficial and hypocritical as there cannot be any spiritual connection between God and an unforgiving spirit. Thus, harbouring an unforgiving attitude will ensure we get cut off from the spirit of God.

No matter who the object of our resentment is or what the offence is, once we welcome and give residence to the unforgiving spirit in our hearts, we do not only grieve the Lord's Spirit, we alienate and bid Him goodbye. Unforgiveness is like a placard reading: HOLY SPIRIT, STAY AWAY. It is a terrible spiritual route to follow.

A Classic Example

A classic example of living a life that is not tainted with resentment is the life of Joseph, the son of Jacob. Joseph was a young man who was hated bitterly by his half-brothers and this was a bitterness that led to all manner of evil being perpetrated against him. The build-up to the hatred and bitterness that his half-brothers, sons of Jacob, had for him appeared to have been conceived from the time when Jacob arrived Haran and fell in love with Rachel, Laban's daughter.

Laban deceived Jacob after serving him for seven years in order to marry Rachel into marrying Leah, his first daughter and Rachel's elder sister. Some animosity built up in Jacob as a result of this fraud as he had to spend another seven years in order to marry his heartthrob, Rachel. Jacob married both sisters.

Leah was very fruitful, giving birth to six sons while her maid and her sister's maid had two sons each. Rachel eventually delivered a son, Joseph. Being the son of his main love, Rachel, and born to him in his old age, Jacob loved Joseph unabashedly to the astonishment of his half-brothers. Jacob did not hide his preference of Joseph over all the other children of his. He made him a coat of many colours to the chagrin of his half-brothers. This discriminatory love Jacob had for Joseph fuelled the hatred of his half-brothers.

Joseph's Dreams

Joseph's dreams did not help matters. He boldly revealed

his dreams of how his siblings and parents bowed before him. This was too much for his half-brothers to bear. They bide their time to deal finally with this dreamer and usurper of their father's love.

Opportunity To Deal With Joseph

When the opportunity to deal with Joseph presented itself, his half-brothers did not fail to grab it with both hands.

Now, consider Joseph heart; even though he was well aware that he was not liked by his half-brothers, he went out of his way to look out for them and to be sure that their welfare was not in jeopardy. He had to search intensely, seeking to find his brothers in order to present them with what his father had given him for them.

On sighting him, his half-brothers were so excited that the opportunity they had been expecting had presented itself to them with little or no difficulty. Their original intent was to kill him and end the story of this one-sided love of their father while truncating his so-called dreams.

But for God's providence, Joseph would have been killed by his half-brothers. They later decided on a lesser evil by selling him to the Ishmaelites.

The Source Of The Hatred Of Joseph's Brothers

In the case of Joseph and his family, we could notice that

there was an endemic flow of this spirit of vengefulness from his fore parents. There was hatred, bitterness, jealousy, anger and revenge in the lives of Sarah, Hagar, Esau and Jacob. Joseph's ten brothers also assumed another dimension of those emotions. It was an ancestral flow stemming from what took place in the lives of Leah, Jacob and Rachael. I am placing Jacob in the middle of the struggle for when we read the account in **Genesis 29:31-35.**

> *"When the Lord saw that Leah was not loved, He opened her womb, but Rachael was barren. Leah became pregnant and gave birth to a son. She named him Reuben, for she said, "It is because the Lord has seen my misery. Surely my husband will love me now." She conceived again, and when she gave birth to a son she said, "Because the Lord heard that I am not loved, He gave me this one too." So she named him Simeon. Again she conceived, and when she gave birth to a son she said, "Now at last my husband will become attached to me, because I have borne him three sons." So he was named Levi. She conceived again, and when she gave birth to a son she said, "THIS TIME I WILL PRAISE THE LORD." So she named him JUDAH. Then she stopped having children. (NIV).*

This is the statement that brings God into Jacob's family and by extension, taught everyone that our personal effort without God will amount to a waste of time and energy. The arm of flesh shall always fail humanity. The naming of her children were coloured by the bitterness of not being loved and she felt that having male children for her husband would cement her marital relationship just as many women think, even now.

WHY SHOULD WE FORGIVE?

This destructive spirit was very much at work that at a point in the account, Leah had to bribe the sister Rachael to have access to sleep with her husband for more procreation. When she was able to give God praise in all situations, the Lord had mercy on her and her family. He will also have mercy on us!

Genesis 30:1,2, says,

> "When Rachael saw that she was not bearing Jacob any children, she became jealous of her sister. So she said to Jacob, "Give me children, or I'll die!" Jacob became angry with her and said, "Am I in the place of God, who has kept you from having children?"

The first three sons carried the weight of bitterness that coloured the fabric of Jacob's family foundation until Leah had to voice out, "THIS TIME, I WILL PRAISE THE LORD! At the birth of her fourth son, Judah. By this statement a positive spiritual frequency was released into force. This frequency in Judah caused him to accept being a SURETY for the family when Joseph had not yet unveiled his identity to his brothers in Egypt. See Genesis 44.

The statement of Joseph came after two full years of struggle in his heart. That statement of forgiveness broke the generational unforgiving pattern, re-united the family of Jacob and formed the foundation for a nation set aside for God.

"Don't be afraid. Am I in the place of God? You intended to harm me, but God intended it for good to accomplish what is now being done, the saving of many lives. So then don't be afraid. I will provide for you and your children.' And he reassured them and spoke kindly to them." Genesis 50:19-21. (NIV).

Joseph, The Prime Minister Of Egypt

There is a classic lesson every believer in Christ needs to learn from the story of Joseph.

The road for Joseph from the pit his brothers threw him into, all the way to the office of the Prime Minister of Egypt, was filled with many dangers and pains. The experiences were well enough to make Joseph perpetually hate his brothers and seek revenge on them when the opportunity came. But being a man full of God's Spirit, he understood that it was God at work. The grievous circumstances he passed through did not becloud his faith. Through it all, God's presence never left him because he did not let himself wallow in self-pity nor become overwhelmed by hatred and bitterness, the forerunners of an unforgiving spirit.

Instead, Joseph saw God in all the situations and circumstances he found himself in; his faith in God could not be shaken. He was at peace with God and himself even under pains of great injustice perpetrated by his brothers, Potiphar's wife and others. No wonder God had pleasure in Him throughout his period of suffering and persecution.

WHY SHOULD WE FORGIVE?

One can see that even though Joseph was a slave, a property in an idolatrous and pagan country, Egypt, he was fully aware of the presence of the living God and did not for once shirk his accountability to his God throughout the period. He would speak again and again of his God without being afraid of the Egyptians or anyone. He always sprinkled his answers to many questions put before him with references to the God he served.

In Genesis chapter 39 verse 9, he said,

>*"How then could I do such a wicked thing and sin against God,"*

in his reply to Potiphar's wife advances. Then in chapter 40 verse 8 of same Genesis, he said

>*"Do not interpretations belong to God?"*

In Genesis 41 verse 16, he said,

>*"I cannot do it, but God will give Pharoah the answer he desires."*

In Genesis 41 verse 25, he again replied to Pharaoh,

>*"God has revealed to Pharaoh what He is about to do"*

and in Genesis 41 verse 32 again in his response to Pharoah, he said,

"The matter has been firmly decided by God and God will do it soon."

This showed a man who though in great pains, temptations and dangers never lost sight of God. Notwithstanding all the injustices perpetrated against him, his eyes were upon God and on God alone. He could see God in everything that was happening to him. He could see the hand of God in all the problems, in all the temptations and evils that came upon him he did not see the perpetrators of these injustices and evils against him. He did not see them at all. All his gaze was on God, even in those situations. This was because he knew that God had a hand in his life and so, he could not take his eyes away from God.

In every situation, he was quick to invoke God as the Almighty, omnipresent God, and the One who knows all things, holds all things and can do all things. It was easy therefore for him in every situation to know that God was taking him through a journey and that the end of the journey would surely be a good one.

So, beloved in Christ, it is important that we understand that what you are passing through right now, God knows about it and He knows that the end thereof will be to your benefit if you will only get bitterness out of your system and allow God bring to pass that which he has purposed for your life and for which he allowed this very situation come your way.

WHY SHOULD WE FORGIVE?

Joseph Forgives His Brothers

Chapter 45 of the book of Genesis is a classic example of forgiving one another. It is also a reminder to us that God's love for us transcends all we are passing through, no matter what it is or the cause of it. It brings to light the truth of Romans chapter 8 verse 28 that God is at work in all things happening to us who believe in him with the purpose of bringing us to a good end.

Although Joseph put his brothers to some tests to prove if they have been cured of their jealousy, envy and bitterness, his greatest interest was for his brothers to see what he passed through as having God's hand in it. That it was a means which God used in saving the family of Jacob at this crucial time of famine.

His brothers, at this point, showed remorse for their past behaviour and lack of concern for their father's well-being. It is evident at this point that God had also touched them. They were more cohesive and looked out for one another. This showed in Judah, son of Leah's decision to volunteer and sincerely too, ask to be taken into prison instead of Benjamin, son of Rachel.

This is a salient point to note in the transformation that had taken place in them. Judah could not bear to see his father in pains again after all that Jacob had passed through when they deceived him by telling him that Joseph had been killed by wild animals. Judah could not bear to see his father pass through such pains again and so, he volunteered for the sake of his father and for the sake of his younger brother even though Benjamin was his step-brother. He decided to bear the brunt of whatsoever punishment that was meant for Benjamin. What a great transformation!

Although Joseph was pleased at the transformation that had taken place in his brothers, I believe his forgiveness of his brothers was a fruit of his relationship with God rather than the changes he had noticed in them.

Forgiveness is divine. Therefore, we need a divine touch to be able to forgive. Once our mind is stayed on God, the Lord Jesus who forgave his tormentors while on the cross, will empower us with the same Spirit that he had to enable us forgive those who have badly offended us. We need his grace (which, of course, is in abundance) to be able to forgive. It is the only way to achieve forgiveness. That is the only way. We have to rely on Christ, look up to Him and ask for grace to forgive no matter how terribly we are offended.

No matter how much the bitterness that has built up in you, our Lord Jesus can give you both the grace and the power to forgive and move on with your life. Life is too precious to be ruined with an unforgiving spirit.

It is Christ-like to forgive. In the same vein, it is satan-like not to forgive. Let us be like our Master, our God and our Saviour, even our Lord Jesus who forgave us so much and

WHY SHOULD WE FORGIVE?

gave his life to redeem us. He shed his blood that we may have salvation. He forgave us of all the terrible things we have done and has brought us into the kingdom of God. He made us His brothers (Hebrews 2: 10-12) and one with Himself. Why can't we then seek His grace and this same Spirit of forgiveness from Him to enable us forgive?

Maybe you need to forgive your spouse, your father, your mother, your siblings or your uncles. It could be someone at your work place or business place, your nosey neighbour, those that hate you or somebody who has offended you so badly, learn from Christ and forgive. Christ forgave you and forgave me, too. Let us be like Christ and forgive as He forgave us, for forgiveness is divine. Amen.

CHAPTER 16

WHAT SHOULD BE OUR RESPONSE TO HURTS AND OFFENSES?
"There's forgiveness amongst decent people."

The LORD laid an example for us to follow. While on the Cross, our LORD prayed,

> *"Father forgive them, for they do not know what they do."* (Luke 23:34).

Our LORD KNEW THE SOURCE OF HIS TORMENT. He knew that the enemy was behind the work of those who crucified Him.
That was why in teaching HIS disciples to pray, He was emphatic in verse 4 of Luke 11: 1-4 that we should ask GOD to

> *"forgive us our sins, as we also forgive everyone who is indebted to us".*

Our forgiveness of those who offend us should be without exception for if not, our Father in Heaven will not forgive us but will give us over to the tormentor to torment us in perpetuity.
Daniel 9:9 says that

> *"To the LORD our GOD belong mercy and forgiveness, though we rebelled against HIM."*

However, GOD's forgiveness of our sins is consequent upon our forgiving those who sinned against us no matter how grievous the offence seems (Luke 11:4; Mathew 18:34,35).
Prov.17:9 says

that he who forgives a transgression seeks love.

GOD is Love and he who seeks love seeks the Life of GOD.

To err is human but to forgive is divine, to seek love in the face of being transgressed against is surely divine. When we forgive, especially when we are shamed and disgraced, we show a rare level of maturity propelled by divine life that is flowing in us. You cannot say you are spiritually mature and yet live an unforgiving life, full of a strong passion for revenge or even worse, desire evil to befall him who has offended you.

You cannot hurt GOD's anointed and be free; no, it is not possible. We should bear in mind that every born again Christian is carrying CHRIST THE ANOINTED ONE. That makes us anointed children of GOD. IF YOU HURT ANY OF THESE, NO MATTER HOW GRIEVOUSLY YOU MAY HAVE BEEN OFFENDED, YOU SURELY WILL NOT GO FREE.

The LORD desires us to be like Him, to have a heart that seeks love in the face of transgression against us. We who were once in great darkness as a result of our transgressions against the LORD, He forgave and brought us out of darkness into His marvellous light. (I Peter 2:9; Acts 26:18)

God's Word Edition of the Bible translated Prov. 14:9 like this,

> *"There's forgiveness amongst decent people."*

Surely, there's forgiveness amongst decent people. Anyone with a heart full of unforgiveness carries a darkened heart and therefore, cannot be a decent person. A heart full of bitterness and a desire for revenge is apparently an indecent heart that is devoid of Christ and all He stands for.

In Eph.4:31-32, the scripture says,

> *"Let all bitterness, wrath, anger, clamour, and evil speaking be put away from you, with all malice. And be kind to one another, tender-hearted, forgiving one another, even as GOD in CHRIST forgave you."*

John MacArthur[3] in his footnotes of the above verses in **The MACARTHUR** Study Bible stated thus:

These two verses summarize the changes expected in the life of a believer.
"Bitterness" reflects a smothering resentment. "Wrath" has to do with rage- a passion of the moment. "Anger" is a more internal, deep hostility. "Clamour" is the outcry of strife beyond control. "Evil speaking" is slander. "Malice" is the

general Greek term for evil, the root of all vices. These vices are normally the outcome of a heart full of an unforgiving attitude. Contrary to possessing and expressing an unforgiving heart, these verses encourage us as those who have been forgiven so much by GOD, to forgive the relatively small offenses done against us by others. The most graphic illustration of this truth is the parable of Mathew 18:21-35.

Following in the same trend Paul in Col.3:12,13 said that

> "Therefore, as the elect of GOD, holy and beloved, put on tender mercies, kindness, humility, meekness, longsuffering; bearing with one another, if anyone has a complaint against another; even as CHRIST forgave you, so you also must do."

Brethren, it is not optional, it is a MUST-DO TO FORGIVE. John MacArthur[4] in his footnotes on the above explained that:

> 'elect of GOD designates true Christians as those who have been chosen by GOD. No one is converted solely by his own choice, but only in response to GOD'S effectual, free, uninfluenced, and sovereign grace. Beloved. Election means believers are the objects of GOD's incomprehensible special love'.

Beloved we are special before GOD. HE gave HIS best to bring us in. Will HE therefore be asking too much by requiring us as believers to emulate CHRIST? CHRIST as the model of forgiveness has forgiven all our sins totally (Col. 1:14; 2:13,14), should we as believers not follow in HIS footsteps and be willing without let to forgive others that offended us? We surely must come to terms with this fact that no one who professes CHRIST and still holds on to unforgiveness is a true disciple of the LORD.

LOOK AT THE LIVES OF THOSE WE CONSIDERED IN THIS BOOK. THE END RESULT IS SELF-DESTRUCTION AND THE OUTER DARKNESS.

James 2:13 says

> *"For he shall have judgement without mercy, that hath shewed no mercy; and mercy rejoiceth against judgement"* *(KJV)*

Today, the LORD is ministering to you to release all those you have locked up in the prison yard of your heart. Open your heart, seek for love by forgiving them no matter how grievous you might perceive what was done to you. May the good LORD save us from the place of torment by granting us the grace to forgive all that offended us. Amen.

We need to be proactive. You need to stand up right away at the end of reading this book and go or get in touch with those that offended you. Let him or her know you were offended by his or her actions but that the Good LORD has healed you now and you have forgiven him or her from the depths of your heart.

SAVE YOURSELF FROM IMPENDING DANGER! DO IT NOW TOMORROW MAY BE TOO LATE.

WHAT SHOULD BE OUR RESPONSE TO HURTS AND OFFENSES?

MAY GOD BLESS YOU FOR READING THIS BOOK. AMEN.

NOTES

[1]Matthew Henry's Concise Commentary on the Bible
http://www.ccel.org/ccel/henry/mhcc.html
Grand Rapids, MI: Christian Classics Ethereal Library
Logos Research Systems, Inc.
Genesis Chapter 4 verses 19 to 24

[2] GotQuestions.org ONLINE:
"Who were the sons of Korah in the Old Testament?"

[3] John MacArthur
The   JOHN MACARTHUR STUDY BIBLE
THOMAS NELSONS BIBLES
A Division of Thomas Nelson, Inc
www.ThomasNelson.com
Footnotes on Ephesians 4: 31, 32

[4] John MacArthur
The   JOHN MACARTHUR STUDY BIBLE
THOMAS NELSONS BIBLES
A Division of Thomas Nelson, Inc
www.ThomasNelson.com
Footnotes on Colosians 3: 12, 1

ABOUT THE AUTHOR

Dr Chibueze Ukaegbu, a graduate of the prestigious Imperial College, London, trained as a Chemical Engineer and a Management Scientist. He is a Fellow of the Nigerian Institute of Management.

After a stint with the private sector, Dr Ukaegbu joined the Abia State of Nigeria Civil Service in 1993, from where he retired after twenty one years of meritorious service to the State. He reached the peak of his career with his appointment as a Permanent Secretary in the Abia State Public Service in the year 2006. A position he held for over six years before retiring from Service in the year 2013.

Dr Chibueze Ukaegbu gave his life to CHRIST in 1970. Ever since then he has served His Lord in various capacities in the Church of the Living God. His entire life revolves around CHRIST AND THE CHURCH.

He is married with six grown up children and eight grand children. His children, all born-again, are serving the Lord in different capacities all over the world.

Dr Chibueze Ukaegbu is presently channelling all his energies in writing books that will contribute in the building of the Church. He is also a Consultant Management Scientist.

For Additional Help Or Comments, Please Contact The Author:
info@drchibuezeukaegbu.com

THE FRUIT OF UNFORGIVENESS

Printed in Great Britain
by Amazon

82699548R00133